C000174043

The
GREAT WESTERN
REVIVAL

The
GREAT WESTERN REVIVAL

ADDRESSES
of
HIS HOLINESS
MIRZA MASROOR AHMAD

KHALIFATUL-MASIH V[ABA]
HEAD OF THE WORLDWIDE AHMADIYYA
MUSLIM COMMUNITY

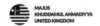

MAJLIS
KHUDDAMUL AHMADIYYA
UNITED KINGDOM

The Great Western Revival

Addresses of

His Holiness Mirza Masroor Ahmad,

Khalifatul-Masih V[aba]

(Fifth Successor to the Promised Messiah[as])

Head of the Worldwide Ahmadiyya Muslim Community

First Edition Published 2020

Reprinted 2021

© Majlis Khuddamul Ahmadiyya UK

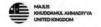

Published by

Majlis Khuddamul Ahmadiyya UK

Unit 2, Bourne Mill Business Park, Guildford Road,

Farnham, Surrey, UK, GU9 9PS

www.khuddam.org.uk

www.thegreatrevival.co.uk

Printed and bound by CPI Group (UK) Ltd, Croydon. CR0 4YY

Photos © Makhzan-e-Tasaweer

ISBN: 978-1-8381429-0-2

10 9 8 7 6 5 4 3 2 1

"

God desires of you no more than
that you deal equitably with all people
and show kindness even to those
who have not done you any good.
More importantly, you ought to love
God's creation as if it were your kith
and kin, in the same manner that
mothers treat their children.

— Noah's Ark
Hazrat Mirza Ghulam Ahmad - the Promised Messiah[as]

Contents

About His Holiness Khalifatul-Masih V^{aba}

His Holiness, Hazrat Mirza Masroor Ahmad, Khalifatul-Masih V^{aba} [Caliph of the Messiah], is the supreme head of the worldwide Ahmadiyya Muslim Community. He is the fifth successor to the Promised Messiah and Reformer, Hazrat Mirza Ghulam Ahmad^{as} of Qadian.

The holy office of the Khalifatul-Masih was established in 1908 after the demise of the founder of the Ahmadiyya Muslim Community. The role of the Khalifatul-Masih is to further the cause of the Promised Messiah^{as} whom Ahmadi Muslims believe to be the prophet of the latter days, as foretold and awaited by the majority of religions today.

His Holiness was born on 15 September 1950 in Rabwah, Pakistan to the late respected Mirza Mansoor Ahmad and the late respected Nasirah Begum Ahmad. Upon completing his Masters Degree in Agricultural Economics in 1977 from the Agriculture University in Faisalabad, Pakistan, he formally dedicated his life to the service of Islam. He was sent to Ghana in 1977, where for several years he served as a principal of various Ahmadiyya Muslim schools.

Later, when His Holiness returned to Pakistan, he served in various capacities at the Headquarters of the Ahmadiyya Community in Rabwah. In 1999, owing to anti-Ahmadiyya laws in Pakistan, His Holiness was imprisoned for a short period of time on the false charge of erasing words of the Holy Qur'an from a sign.

Elected to the lifelong position of Khalifah (Caliph) of the Ahmadiyya Muslim Community on 22 April 2003, His Holiness serves as the worldwide spiritual and administrative head of an international religious organisation with tens of millions of members spread across more than 200 countries.

Since being elected as the Khalifatul-Masih, His Holiness has led a worldwide campaign to convey the peaceful message of Islam, through all forms of print and digital media. Under his leadership, national branches of the Ahmadiyya Muslim Community have launched campaigns that reflect the true and peaceful teachings of Islam. Ahmadi Muslims around the world are engaged in grassroot efforts to convey a message of peace to Muslims and non-Muslims alike, host interfaith and peace symposia, and present exhibitions of the Holy Qur'an to disseminate its true and noble message. These campaigns have received worldwide media coverage and demonstrate that Islam champions peace, loyalty to one's country of residence and service to humanity.

In 2004, His Holiness launched the Peace Symposium in which guests from all walks of life come together to exchange ideas on the promotion of peace and harmony. Each year the symposium attracts many serving ministers, parliamentarians, politicians, religious leaders and other dignitaries.

His Holiness has travelled around the world to promote and facilitate service to humanity. He has delivered addresses at various parliaments with the underlying message being one of fostering an atmosphere of peace and religious harmony.

Under the leadership of His Holiness, the Ahmadiyya Muslim Community has built a number of schools and hospitals that provide excellent education and healthcare facilities in remote parts of the world.

His Holiness strives to establish peace at every level of society. He constantly advises members of the Ahmadiyya Muslim Community to carry out a Jihad of self-reformation, which is the true and most significant form of Jihad.

Millions around the world seek the guidance and counsel of His Holiness in matters related to every aspect of life.

His Holiness, Mirza Masroor Ahmad[aba] currently resides in England. As the spiritual leader of Ahmadi Muslims all over the world, he vigorously champions the cause of Islam through a refreshing message of peace and compassion.

Introduction

As mankind tries to settle into the 21st century, challenges continue to appear with more severity and frequency. Political upheavals, economic recessions and social incoherence continue to disturb the equilibrium of the human mind, making it scramble for anything that promises a glimmer of tranquility. Though one would expect that by now, humankind should have learnt all the lessons necessary to – at least – continue along a steady trajectory of peace, this does not appear to be the reality. Once again, similar to the pre-World War era, nations are becoming polarised along the lines of religion, culture and political thought. Policies of division are being adopted across the globe, with its architects overlooking the great cost that will have to be paid as a result. Though such delicate economic, political and social circumstances have perhaps occasioned each nation at some point in its history, what is unique about today is that those conditions are befalling mankind en masse.

It is with this urgent need for peace that we introduce you to an individual who has been tirelessly persistent in pursuing the avenues that lead to harmony. His Holiness, Mirza Masroor Ahmad, Khalifatul-Masih V[aba] and head of the worldwide Ahmadiyya Muslim Community, has been at the heart of a movement trying to motivate change towards resolving the challenges that we face today.

In this collection of six addresses delivered by His Holiness in three European countries, he addresses topics such as Jihad, immigration, the conflicts in the Middle East, social unrest and economic imbalance. He reflects upon true Islamic teachings on a vast range of areas that are of current debate. Furthermore, he not only discusses the Islamic perspective on current affairs but illustrates the Islamic practice that was undertaken by the Founder of Islam: the Holy Prophet Muhammad[sa]. His Holiness dispels common myths about Islam, explaining, describing and drawing upon the history of the religion to show its actual countenance.

For instance, in the address titled *Terrorism Was Never Justified by the Holy Prophet Muhammad [sa]*, delivered at the Peace Symposium 2016 in London, the primary message is not only that Islam is a religion of peace, but that it is also a faith which is anti-extremism. Islam does not support the actions of terrorists who use its teachings as a facade for political gain. His Holiness presents verses of the Holy Qur'an – the basis of Shariah – which explain the methods of establishing peace in great depth. This address gives insight into the Islamic vision of international relations that are built upon the robust foundations of practice established by the Prophet Muhammad[sa].

A common element in many of the addresses delivered by His Holiness is drawing attention to the looming threat of a third world war. In the address titled *True and Sustainable World Peace*, His Holiness highlights the critical need for peace in light of growing tensions and proxy wars that are continually taking aggressive forms.

The UNESCO address stands out as one in which the importance of education in Islam – alongside the value of peace – is discussed at great length. This address is similar to the final chapter of this book titled *Ahmadi Muslim Researchers; Restoring Islam's Golden Age*, delivered at the first international Ahmadiyya Muslim Research Association (AMRA) Conference in the UK. In this address, His Holiness emphasises the need for Ahmadi Muslim academics to excel in their fields for the sake of serving mankind and continuing to find more evidence for the existence of God. His Holiness also explains the reason why Islamic academic prestige, which saw the emergence of the golden age of Islam, declined and what its re-emergence requires.

Where these addresses are filled with references to Islamic teachings, at the same time they serve as a practical guide on how to translate theory into action. We are certain that the words contained in the proceeding pages will have a profound impact on the reader, as those who have been fortunate enough to be part of the audience at such addresses have narrated to us a similar experience.

The Publishers

Notes from the Publisher

References to the Holy Qur'an have been made with *In the name of Allah, the Most Gracious, Ever Merciful,* counted as the first verse. Where the reference of a verse has been quoted in the text of an address, it has not been given as a reference in the *Notes* section.

It is Islamic custom to use honorifics after the names of certain holy individuals. For example, whenever mention is made of the Prophet Muhammad, the letters ^{sa} are superscripted immediately after his name and stand for *sallallahu alayhi wa sallam* (peace and blessings of Allah be upon him) e.g. The Holy Prophet Muhammad^{sa}.

The names of other prophets are followed by ^{as} which is an abbreviation for *alayhis-salam* (peace be upon him).

The names of the companions of the Holy Prophet

Muhammad[sa] or of the Promised Messiah[as] are followed by the letters [ra], which is an abbreviation for *radiyallu anhu/anha* (may Allah be pleased with him/her).

The names of deceased, pious Muslims who are neither companions of the Holy Prophet Muhammad[sa], nor of the Promised Messiah[as], are followed by the letters [rh] which stand for *rahmatullahi alayhi* (may Allah have mercy upon him).

The name of the current Khalifatul-Masih is followed by the letters [aba] which stand for *ayyadahullahu tala bi nasrihil aziz* (may Allah help him with His powerful support).

In some cases, the actual salutations have been set out in full, but wherever this is not the case the abbreviations have been used.

Terrorism was Never Justified *by the* Prophet Muhammad[sa]

13TH NATIONAL PEACE SYMPOSIUM
The Baitul Futuh Mosque, London, UK
19 MARCH 2016

"O people! Spread peace, feed the hungry, and pray at night when people are sleeping and you will enter Paradise in peace"

— The Holy Prophet Muhammad^{sa}

Terrorism was Never Justified *by the* Prophet Muhammad[sa]

Bismillahir Rahmanir Raheem – in the Name of Allah, the Gracious, Ever-Merciful.

Assalamo Alaikum wa Rahmatullah wa Barakatohu – peace and blessings of Allah be upon you all.

First of all I would like to take this opportunity to express my sincere gratitude to all of our distinguished guests who have accepted our invitation and joined us here this evening. Your attendance is particularly noteworthy given that this event is taking place at a time when widespread fear of Islam is on the increase due to the horrific and disgraceful acts of terrorist groups.

For example, last November, the world watched in horror when the terrorist attacks took place in Paris, and apart from this, there have been suicide bombings and attacks in various countries at regular intervals. In terms of the United Kingdom, very recently the Assistant Commissioner of Police warned that Daesh was planning *"enormous and spectacular"* terrorist attacks here in the UK, targeting high-profile and public places.[1]

Furthermore, there has been a sudden influx of refugees into Europe during the past year and this is causing a degree of fear, uncertainty and even panic in the minds of many people. In light of all of this, your attendance and willingness as non-Muslims, to attend an event organised by a Muslim community, proves that you are courageous, tolerant and open-hearted people.

Nonetheless, the simple truth is that there is no need for anyone to fear true Islam. Whilst some people claim Islam to be a religion of extremism and one that promotes suicide attacks or other forms of terrorism, nothing could be further from the truth. Recently, a well-known English columnist wrote about the rise of Islamophobia in a national newspaper. He wrote that he had done extensive research on suicide bombings and found that the first such attack took place in the 1980s, despite the fact that Islam had existed for well over 1300 years. He concluded that if Islam permitted or encouraged such attacks then they ought to have occurred from the outset of Islam and throughout its history.[2] His point was valid and very well made, and proved that such attacks were a modern-day evil, far removed from the true and peaceful teachings of Islam. Certainly, Islam has very clearly prohibited all forms of suicide and so there is no justification whatsoever for suicide attacks or any other forms of terrorism. Such heinous acts lead to the murder and barbaric slaughter of innocent women, children and other members of the public. A recent research article by Dr. Considine of Rice University, in Houston, Texas, clearly says that the persecution of Christians in the so-called Islamic state is not justified by Prophet Muhammad's[sa] writings. It further states that the Prophet's[sa] vision of a Muslim nation was one of religious pluralism and civil rights.[3]

Thus, let it be clear that such acts are absolutely contrary to Islamic teachings. If Islam has ever permitted warfare, it is only to the extent of a defensive war, where war has been forced upon you. For example, in chapter 22, verse 40 of the Holy Qur'an, Allah the Almighty has said that permission for warfare is given to those people upon whom war has been forcibly imposed. In that same verse, Allah the Almighty said that in the case of religious warfare He would help and support those who had been wronged. In early Islam, the wars that took place were genuine religious wars fought for the sake of upholding the fundamental principle of universal religious freedom. History proves that the wars fought with this intention made Muslims victorious, regardless of the fact that a handful of unequipped Muslims fought against

7

huge, well-equipped armies.

However, as a Muslim, when I analyse the wars involving Muslims today, I am certain that they cannot be classed as religious wars. For one, most of the wars taking place in the Muslim world are either internal civil strife or with the neighbouring Muslim countries. Secondly, if ever non-Muslim countries are involved, they have never declared the war as religious and rather helped both sides of Muslims. Thus, present-day wars are not being fought for the sake of Islam or for the sake of religion, but are for economic or geopolitical gains and are proving only a means of defaming Islam's name.

And so based upon what I have just said, I hope it is now clear that there is no need to fear Islam and that it is not a religion of extremism, or one that permits suicide attacks or indiscriminate violence. There is no need for Islamophobia because Islam's true teachings are of peace, tolerance and mutual respect. Islam's teachings are of upholding human values and protecting the honour, dignity and freedoms of all people.

However, of course, we are all well aware that there are some extremists and so-called Islamic groups that are perpetrating the very worst forms of brutality in the name of Islam. Nevertheless, the verse of the Qur'an I quoted earlier makes it clear that such acts are not permitted or justified in any shape or form by Islam.

Another significant matter, which instead of leading me as a Muslim towards warfare and violence, leads me towards exhibiting love for all of humanity, is the fact that in the second verse of the very first chapter of the Holy Qur'an, it is stated that Allah the Almighty is the *"Provider and Sustainer of all the worlds",* and the third verse states that He is the *"Gracious, Ever-Merciful".*[4] Thus, when Allah the Almighty is the Provider and Sustainer of all people and Gracious, Ever-Merciful, how could it be that He desired for those who believed in Him to mercilessly murder, violently oppose or harm His Creation in any way? Of course the answer is that it is not possible. Nonetheless, Allah the Almighty has certainly permitted for action to be taken to stop cruelty, inhumanity and injustice.

Islam states that a Muslim should seek to stop the hand of an oppressor and to end all forms of injustice and transgression.[5] According to Islam there are two ways in which this can be achieved. Firstly, it is far better if peace can be attained through mutual dialogue, negotiations and diplomacy. However, where this is not possible, only then force may be used in order to stop wrongdoing with the intention of establishing sustainable peace.

Outside of the religious context, in every society and nation, there are rules and laws that exist and if they are violated then punitive action is normally taken. If it is possible to reform without punishment or with just a mild sanction or reprimand, that is better; however, if that is not possible then severe punishment is duly discharged for the benefit of the wider society, and as a means of deterrent to others.

Moving to a religious context, according to Islam, punishment or sanction is permitted not as a means of revenge or retribution, but only as a means of ending cruelty or persecution, and as a means of positive reformation. The Holy Qur'an has said that if a person or group can be rehabilitated through forgiveness and mercy then this method should be adopted.[6] However, if clemency or forbearance does not prove effective then punishment should be administered as a means of reformation and improvement. Therefore, the philosophy underpinning punishment in Islam is extremely far-sighted and quite unique. Its purpose is to reform, rehabilitate and improve. It is to develop the highest standards of human values amongst mankind so that, by adopting the attributes of their Creator, all people come to respect and care for one another.

Therefore, where the rights of an individual or group are unjustly usurped, Islam permits punishments that are proportionate to the crime; however, it remains the case that if reformation can be achieved without sanction it is preferable. This is why Allah the Almighty has said in chapter 24, verse 23, of the Holy Qur'an that it is better to forgive and to manifest forbearance.

Similarly, in chapter 3, verse 135, Allah the Almighty has said that those who suppress their anger and who forgive and forget, are those whom Allah loves and prefers. Furthermore, at many other places in the Holy Qur'an, it is stated that a person should forgive wherever possible, because the ultimate purpose is always moral reformation, rather than vengeance. In terms of conflict between nations or groups, Allah the Almighty has given a golden principle for the establishment of long-lasting peace in chapter 49, verse 10, of the Holy Qur'an. In the verse, it states that if there is a dispute between nations or groups, third parties should seek to mediate and to bring about a peaceful resolution to the conflict. In the event of an agreement, all parties should act equitably, but if either party contravenes the settlement and takes aggressive measures, then the other nations or groups should unite together and even use force if necessary to stop the aggressor. However, once the aggressive party withdraws and adopts peace they should not be unduly restricted but should be permitted to move forward as an independent nation and a free society.

Therefore, as the Provider and Sustainer of all of mankind, Allah the Almighty desires for all people to live together in peace and to be free from all forms of persecution and injustice.

In terms of belief, Islam enshrines the principles of universal religious freedom and freedom of conscience.

According to Islam, every person not only has the right of freedom of belief, but also has the right to peacefully propagate their beliefs.

Faith is, and always will be, a matter of the heart and so there should never be any form of compulsion in religion. Whilst Allah the Almighty has deemed Islam to be a complete teaching, no one has the right to forcefully convert others to it. Anyone, whether religious or not, is free to accept Islam, but the key point is that it should be accepted freely and entirely of one's own volition and choice. Similarly, if a Muslim decides that he wishes to leave Islam, then, according to the teachings of the Qur'an, he or she has the right to do so.[7] Whilst we believe Islam to be a universal religion and a timeless teaching, if anyone chooses to leave it then that is their choice and prerogative. In chapter 5, verse 55, Allah says that if anyone wants to leave, let them go. He will replace them with better and sincere ones. No government, group or individual has a right to punish them or sanction them in any way.

Thus, the allegation that Islam mandates punishment for apostasy is entirely unjust and without foundation. Therefore, the teachings of Islam all revolve around Allah and His Being and the fact that He is the Sustainer and Provider for the entire universe. Consequently, if a Muslim seeks to inflict merciless cruelties or to indulge in any forms of extremism then they will have to reject God's attribute of being the Sustainer of all of mankind.

Alternatively, it may be that certain Muslims accept Allah to be the Master of the Universe and the Sustainer of all the Worlds, but have not truly comprehended the meaning of this and have consequently moved far away from Islam's original teachings. Hence, it was to enlighten and educate mankind of the true Islam that we, Ahmadi Muslims, believe that Allah the Almighty sent the Founder of our Community, as the Promised Messiah and Reformer of the Age.

He informed us that the era of religious warfare had come to an end and that God Almighty desired for mankind to live in peace, and to fulfil the rights of their Creator and of one another. Addressing his followers about this, the Promised Messiah, Hazrat Mirza Ghulam Ahmad[as] of Qadian once said:

"According to the true spirit of the teachings of Islam there are only two parts of the religion, or it can be said that the religion is based upon two paramount objectives. First of all is to recognise the One God with absolute certainty and to sincerely love Him and to submerge yourself entirely in His obedience, as per the demands of love and submission. The second purpose is to serve His people and to utilise all of your capabilities and faculties in the loving service of others, and to always show sincere gratitude to whoever is kind to you and to favour them in return, whether they be your monarch or ruler, or whether they be the most simple

and humble of people. And you should always keep a loving bond with them." [8]

Furthermore, the Founder of the Ahmadiyya Muslim Community, has also explained the true meaning of chapter 16, verse 91, of the Holy Qur'an, in which Allah the Almighty states:

"Verily, Allah enjoins justice, and the doing of good to others; and giving like kindred."

The Founder of the Ahmadiyya Muslim Community states that in this verse Muslims are commanded by Allah to be just and fair towards all others. Therefore, Muslims are commanded to be kind and to extend favour to all other people, including those who have not been sympathetic to them or favoured them in any way. Finally, he explained that the verse required a Muslim to love God's creation to such an extent that they considered every person in the world to be like their own close family member.

In fact, he said that a true Muslim should love others, irrespective of their background or belief, in the same way that a mother loves her child. Certainly, this is the highest and purest form of love because in terms of the second stage, where a person exhibits kindness or favour, it is possible that an element of self-projection remains, whether covert

14

or overt, and at some point, the individual may remind the person of their gesture and seek favour in return.

However, a mother's love is truly selfless and altruistic, and her unique bond with her child is such that she is willing to sacrifice everything for the sake of her offspring. She desires nothing in return and nor does she require any form of praise or tribute. Therefore, this is the ultimate standard that Islam advocates, whereby Muslims are taught to love all of humanity as a mother loves her child. These are the true teachings of Islam.[9]

Allah the Almighty has said that those who believe in Him should adopt His attributes[10] and so, it is impossible for a true Muslim to be cruel and it is similarly impossible for Islam to permit any form of injustice, violence or extremism. Over the years, I have made these points time and time again, and have highlighted these core Islamic teachings.

I have repeatedly quoted the Holy Qur'an to prove that what I am saying is based on Islam's authentic teachings. However, it remains that our peaceful and inclusive message is not covered extensively in the media, whilst on the other hand those relatively few people involved in brutality and carnage are given non-stop worldwide media coverage and attention.

There is no doubt that the media plays a huge role in influencing public opinion and so the media should use this power responsibly – as a force for good and as a force for peace. It should show the world what true Islam represents, rather than focusing on the merciless acts of a minority.

Publicity is the oxygen sustaining most terrorist or extremist groups and so, I have no doubt that if the media takes on board what I have said, we will soon find that the terrorism and violence afflicting the world will begin to die away. Personally, I cannot comprehend how the extremists who have plagued Islam and violated its noble teachings can seek to justify their hateful acts in its name.

Islam's teachings of peace prohibit all forms of extremism, to the extent that even in a state of legitimate war, Allah has commanded that any action or punishment should remain proportionate to the crimes committed, and that it is better if patience and forgiveness is manifest. Thus, all those so-called Muslims who are engaged in violence, injustice and brutality are inviting God's wrath and anger to their doorstep.

At a time when fear of Islam is ever increasing, let me stress again that the Holy Qur'an has repeatedly enjoined love, compassion and benevolence. If in certain extreme circumstances the Qur'an permitted defensive warfare, it was only in order to establish peace. Today, we observe that the majority of governments or groups, whether Muslims or non-Muslims, involved in warfare also claim that they are fighting for the sake of establishing peace.

In terms of perception, it seems that most people are

willing to overlook the wars conducted by certain world powers or at least not affiliate their actions to any religion or belief. However, as we live in a climate in which Islam's teachings are being targeted, we see that all cruelties or wars carried out by Muslims are immediately linked to the teachings of Islam. Yet the voices of those people and those groups who are earnestly striving to spread Islam's true and peaceful teachings are not being heard, and not being widely publicised. In my opinion this is unjust and extremely counter-productive. At a time of worldwide conflict, we should remember this basic principle that it is better for all forms of evil and cruelty to be suppressed and for all forms of goodness and humanity to be endorsed. In this way, evil will not spread far, whilst virtue and peace will spread far and wide and adorn our society.

If we promote the good that is happening in the world, we can overcome those who seek to undermine our cherished values of mercy and humanity. Yet the world does not seem to have accepted or understood this principle and that is why the media continues to prioritise its circulation or viewing figures over and beyond the peace of the world. The media, which gladly focuses on the tiny minority involved in brutality, are feeding the propaganda machines of evil groups such as Daesh, yet they fail in their duty to highlight all that is good in the world. This is an injustice that is sowing the seeds of further division and conflict.

In terms of world politics and defeating terrorism, it is necessary to accept that establishing peace is our paramount objective and so, compromise from all sides is required. In case you do not trust the words of a Muslim, let me present to you the views of eminent non-Muslims who are well-versed in political affairs and who desire peace in the world. For example, when speaking about how to defeat extremism and in particular the terrorist group Daesh, Austria's Foreign Minister recently said:

> *"We need a pragmatic common approach in this respect, including the involvement of President Al-Assad in the fight against Islamic State terror. In my opinion the priority is the fight against terror. This will not be possible without powers such as Russia and Iran."* [11]

Further, Professor John Gray, a retired political philosopher who taught for many years at the London School of Economics, recently wrote about the importance of prioritising peace over the type of political system in place. He wrote:

> *"The form of government – democratic, despotic, monarchical or republican – is less important than the capacity to deliver peace."* [12]

In my opinion, this was an extremely insightful comment, yet the world's major powers have continued to prioritise regime change in countries that were previously relatively stable.

For example, the West was determined to remove Saddam Hussein from Iraq and the painful consequences of that war 13 years ago continue to be felt to this day. Another prominent example is Libya, whereby President Gaddafi was forcibly removed from office in 2011 and ever since, Libya has spiralled into a state of lawlessness and unbridled chaos.

A direct consequence of the political vacuum in Libya has been the fact that Daesh has now built a significant base and terror network in the country, which it is continuing to strengthen. The situation is now extremely dangerous, not only for the region, but also for Europe and this is something that I warned of some years ago. Therefore, the priority in such countries should not be regime change for the sake of it. Rather, it should be to ensure that the members of the public are given their due rights and for long-term peace to be established.

Going back to Syria, I agree with the Austrian Foreign Minister when he says that the overriding objective should be to establish peace. Hence, the major powers should be willing to open the channels of communication with Syria's Government and to seek the help of other neighbouring countries that have influence in the region.

Remember, positive change is only possible if one is

willing to set aside their personal interests for the greater good and is willing to act fairly at all times. As I have already said, Islam says that justice is the foundation upon which peace is built. And so we must pay heed to the urgent issues of our time. For many years I have warned that the world is moving rapidly towards another world war and now others are reaching the same conclusion. In fact, some prominent people are now saying that they believe that a world war has already begun. Nonetheless, I believe that we still have the time to stop such a war in its tracks but the solution remains, as I have already said, to act with justice and to leave aside all vested interests.

On a number of previous occasions, I have spoken about the critical importance of cutting the funding and supply lines of extremist groups. Yet it cannot be said that full efforts are being made in this regard. For example, a recent special investigative report published by The Wall Street Journal stated that Daesh was acquiring huge quantities of U.S. dollars from auctions being held by Iraq's central bank. Those same dollars were being provided to Iraq directly from the Federal Reserve in the United States. The article stated that the U.S. Government had known about this since at least June 2015, but personally I believe that world powers knew about such trading for much longer.[13]

Furthermore, in terms of the sale of oil, it is well-known that different groups and even governments are purchasing oil from Daesh. Why has this trade not been stopped? Why have comprehensive sanctions not been imposed to prevent such deals? It seems that when it comes to acquiring oil, morality goes out of the window. This is a point that was also made by Professor Leif Wenar of King's College London in a recent article. He argues that the world tolerates all forms of atrocities for the sake of gaining oil. Thus, countries have bought oil from Daesh and from Sudan where a lot of human rights abuses have taken place. This is a violation of proper fundamental market economics – whereby violence should not create property rights.

Furthermore, in a recent article, the Director of the Iraq Energy Institute explained how Daesh was selling its oil. The author wrote:

> *"Crude oil is transported by tankers to Jordan via Anbar province, to Iran via Kurdistan, to Turkey via Mosul, to Syria's local market and to the Kurdistan region of Iraq, where most of it gets refined locally. It defies logic to say that state officials are not complicit in this trade."* [14]

Therefore, whilst it is claimed that all possible efforts are being made to eradicate terrorism and extremism, the evidence does not substantiate this claim. Given all of this, how can it be said that there is true justice in the world? How can it be claimed that honesty and integrity are considered paramount?

Similarly, recently there has been widespread media coverage documenting the global arms trade. According to official reports, last year the United States exported weapons worth $46.6 billion dollars, which was an increase of more than $12 billion dollars from the previous year. It was further reported that the majority of those weapons were sold to countries in the Middle East and in turn they were fuelling the wars in Syria, Iraq and Yemen.[15] I reiterate that if such trading is taking place, how is it possible for justice and peace to be established?

These few examples I have cited are all in the public domain and are the views of respected analysts and commentators. Until principles of justice are exhibited at all levels of society and between nations, we will not see true peace in the world. Without justice it could take decades to defeat the evil that is Daesh and other extremist groups.

However, if the world heeds this message and comes to manifest justice, and genuine efforts are made to restrict the funding and supply lines of terrorism then I believe – unlike a retired American military general who recently said the war against Daesh will last between 10 and 20 years[16] – that the networks of terrorism tormenting the world can be destroyed imminently.

In conclusion, it is my belief that unless the world comes to recognise its Creator and accepts Him as the Sustainer of mankind, true justice cannot prevail. Not only will true justice not prevail, but we will also experience a lethal nuclear war whose catastrophic consequences will be faced by our future generations. I pray that the world comes to understand this reality. I pray that we all play our respective roles in furthering the cause of humanity. And I pray that true peace, based upon justice, is established in all parts of the world. With these words I would like to once again take the opportunity to thank all of our guests for joining us this evening.

May Allah bless you all. Thank you very much.

Muslim Migrants *and* Integration

ANNUAL CONVENTION OF
THE AHMADIYYA MUSLIM COMMUNITY GERMANY
Karlsruhe, Germany
8 SEPTEMBER 2018

"A true Muslim is he from whose tongue and hand all others are safe."

— The Holy Prophet Muhammad[sa]

Muslim Migrants *and* Integration

Bismillahir Rahmanir Raheem – in the Name of Allah, the Gracious, Ever-Merciful. All distinguished guests, *Assalamo Alaikum Wa Rahmatullahe Wa Barakatohu* – peace and blessings of Allah be upon you all.

In recent times here in Germany, and in several other Western countries, the far-right has gained prominence and seen its membership rise. The root cause for this distressing trend is that the indigenous citizens in these nations are becoming increasingly resentful and frustrated. They are feeling neglected as though their rights are not being protected by their leaders and governments.

Unquestionably, a major factor fuelling their anxiety has been the influx of immigrants to many Western nations in recent years. This has certainly been the case here in Germany, which has taken far more refugees than any other European country in recent times. As a result, many local people are afraid that their societies are changing beyond comprehension and they feel that their nation's resources are being disproportionately utilised in favour of immigrants.

Whilst the term immigrant is used, the real issue for most people is Islam and the fact that the vast majority of immigrants to Europe are Muslims fleeing from war-torn countries in the Middle East. Thus, when the far-right and their supporters raise rallying calls against immigration, their actual target is Islam and their objective is to stop Muslims from entering their nations. They view Islam as incompatible with Western values, and strive to propagate their belief that Muslims are unable to successfully integrate into the West and are a threat to other citizens.

Further, many non-Muslims believe Islam to be a religion of extremism and imagine that those Muslims who immigrate will be extremists or religious fanatics, will spread poison in society, incite division and disturb the peace and well-being of their nation. Certainly, this sense of alarm has spread to some parts of this country, especially in Eastern Germany. Thus, there have been moves and campaigns to ban the building of mosques.

We, the Ahmadiyya Muslim Community, have not been immune to such opposition, whereby some groups here in Germany have actively campaigned against us and endeavoured to stop us building new mosques. They have campaigned against us, even though our motto is *Love for All, Hatred for None*, and despite the fact that for almost 130 years, our community has been at the very forefront of promoting peace, brotherhood, love and compassion in all parts of the world. Our history testifies to the fact that wherever we have built mosques or become established, the fears of the local people have soon evaporated. Those who initially viewed us with suspicion have quickly become our loyal friends and sincere supporters. Throughout the world, our neighbours happily attest to the fact that Ahmadi Muslims are people who promote peace in society and who spread only a message of love, compassion and human sympathy. Yet, due to the dire state of the Muslim world at large, the Ahmadiyya Muslim Community has also had to suffer the consequences.

Another charge raised by those opposed to widespread immigration is that immigrants are prone to sexually abusing or harassing women. Sadly, a recent report suggested that a high proportion of rapes or attempted rapes, in one Western country, were committed by immigrants.[1] God knows better if the figures are accurate, but when such reports are made public, it affects other nations as well and the concerns and fears of local people continue to rise.

Another point that many parties and politicians have focused upon is the tax burden required to re-settle immigrants. Aside from their day-to-day living expenses, infrastructure costs resulting from large-scale immigration are vast and so, the financial burden on the state is considerable and it is ultimately taxpayers who fund this. People who have lived their lives and paid their taxes in a country, are justified to ask whether it is fair that their contributions to the state are spent on resettling foreign immigrants, as opposed to funding projects that are beneficial to existing citizens. I do not dispute that these are valid issues and real causes of concern and, if they are not dealt with wisely, tensions in society will continue to increase.

Additionally, wherever there is large-scale migration, it inevitably leads to security issues. Indeed, it has been proven that hidden amongst the genuine refugees are immigrants who have the potential to cause great harm. For example, just a few days ago, a female refugee living in Germany, who in the past had been kidnapped and kept as a slave in Iraq, was interviewed. She told how she was shocked and horrified to see that her captor, a member of a terrorist group, was now also living freely in Germany, having come here under the pretence of persecution.[2] This is something I have warned about in the past, that each case should be carefully analysed to ensure that extremists or criminals posing as refugees are not allowed to enter.[3] Anyway, these issues mean that a fear of mass immigration from Muslim countries is, to some extent, justified.

Yet, on the other side, it is necessary for a fair-minded, intelligent and wise person to look at both sides of the story and not just base his or her impression of Muslims and Islam upon hearsay. Merely because someone brands Islam a religion of extremism or claims that all Muslims are terrorists does not make it true; rather, it is vital to assess the facts rationally and objectively before reaching a conclusion. Hence, before reaching a definitive conclusion about whether Islam's teachings are of an extremist nature, you should investigate and see what the truth is. Analyse, whether the wicked acts of some so-called Muslims are motivated by the teachings of Islam? Consider, whether Islam really does permit extremism? Or does it prescribe severe punishments for those who spread disorder and hatred? Does Islam permit Muslims to break the laws of the land in the name of their faith? What expectations does Islam place upon Muslims in terms of their conduct in society? Does Islam encourage Muslims to burden the State? Or does it encourage them to work hard, to be loyal and to contribute positively to the society in which they live?

If it is proven that Muslims who do wrong are motivated by their religion, it can be said that the concerns of the far-right are justified. Yet, what if their actions have nothing to do with Islam? What if anti-Islamic groups are spreading hateful myths that are based only on fantasy rather than fact? In the short time available, I will mention a few points that,

33

I hope, will help answer some of these questions and enable you to understand the true essence of Islamic teachings.

Firstly, a basic Islamic principle is that where a Muslim aspires to live peacefully, he must also endeavour to provide peace and security to others. People often speak of the wars fought in early Islam and suggest that they prove that Islam is a bloodthirsty religion that permits force and compulsion. Yet, in reality, the early Muslims endured thirteen years of brutal and sustained persecution without retaliating in any way. Only after that long period did Allah the Almighty permit them to defend themselves and this permission is mentioned in chapter 22, verses 40 to 41 of the Holy Qur'an. In these verses, Allah the Almighty said that those who had been persecuted and driven out of their homes were permitted to defend themselves from further cruelty and oppression. However, the Holy Qur'an further states that if the Muslims did not defend their religion then churches, temples, synagogues, mosques and all other places of worship would all be in grave danger. So, permission was granted to protect the rights of all people to live their lives freely and according to their beliefs.

Muslims are often blamed for extremism. But fair-minded and intelligent people should first investigate these claims to assess whether or not they are true.

In chapter 10, verse 100 of the Holy Qur'an, whilst addressing the Holy Prophet of Islam[sa], Allah the Almighty states that if He desired He could have enforced His will and compelled everyone to accept Islam. However, instead, Allah the Almighty preferred free will to prevail. Likewise, in chapter 18, verse 30 of the Holy Qur'an, Allah the Almighty states that Muslims should openly preach their message and proclaim Islam to be a truthful religion, yet at the same time the Qur'an also states that every person is free to accept or reject it. The verse states:

"Let him who will, believe and let him who will, disbelieve."

In the Holy Qur'an, Allah the Almighty also refers to those non-Muslims who admitted that Islam was a peaceful and benevolent religion, yet they refused to accept it because they feared that embarking upon a path of peace and compassion would harm their material interests. Chapter 28, verse 58 of the Holy Qur'an states:

"And they say, 'If we were to follow the guidance with thee, we should be snatched away from our land'."

This is the true picture of Islam. It requires every Muslim to live peacefully and to contribute to their society. Unquestionably, those Muslims who claim Jihad means to attack non-Muslims or to forcefully convert them, are manifestly wrong. Such beliefs and attitudes have nothing to do with the teachings of Islam.

Another accusation levelled at Islam, which I mentioned earlier, relates to the treatment of women. Some non-Muslims fear that if Muslims migrate to the West they will prey upon the local women and abuse them. Indeed, some immigrants have been guilty of such crimes and their shameful conduct has perpetuated such fears and anxiety. Given this, let me make it categorically clear that any Muslim who violates the honour of a woman or abuses her in any way is acting entirely against Islam's teachings. Islam considers such behaviour as evil and has mandated exceptionally strong punishments for those guilty of such immoral and reprehensible crimes. For example, Islam decrees that if a Muslim is guilty of such a crime, he should be openly flogged in a public setting.[4] Thus, if you truly wish to root out such behaviour, then Muslim men guilty of such abhorrent crimes should be punished according to Islamic law. Although, I am sure Western governments would frown upon this idea and human rights activists would certainly object.

As I said earlier, another major concern for existing citizens is that hosting refugees is a huge financial undertaking by the state. In this regard, no immigrant should enter another nation with a sense of entitlement; rather, they should ponder over what they can offer the local society. I have said many times before that immigrants should consider themselves indebted to the nation that has accepted them.[5]

They owe gratitude to both the government and the public and the way to repay this favour is that they should not waste time seeking only benefits and allowances from the state; rather, they should seek to contribute to the society as soon as possible. They should work hard and strive to enter employment, even if the only job they can get is basic labour work. Where this will enable them to maintain their personal honour and dignity, it will also be a means of relieving the burden on the state and removing the frustrations of the local people.

Certainly, every Muslim should keep in mind that the Holy Prophet of Islam[sa] said that the giving hand is far greater than the one that takes.[6] On many occasions, people sought to help his companions, but they refused to accept and preferred to earn a living for themselves.[7]

As I said, even if refugees are forced to do menial or basic jobs, which they consider themselves over-qualified for, it is better than remaining idle and expecting the state to cover all their needs. Otherwise, immigrants who fail to contribute to society will be a means of increasing restlessness amongst the wider population. Furthermore, if governments do provide some benefits or financial aid to immigrants, they should ensure that they do not neglect the needs of the local people. In some countries, immigrants received better benefits than tax-paying citizens and this led to a natural agitation amongst the public.

Such frustrations do not dissipate on their own because where there is frustration there is always a reaction. Therefore, every government should implement sensible and fair policies that keep in mind the rights and requirements of citizens and immigrants alike, rather local citizens should be given better treatment and benefits.

A few days ago, it was reported that the German Government was considering a new policy whereby asylum seekers would be required to do a year's community service upon settling in Germany.[8] Some critics are already claiming that this is merely a form of *"cheap labour"* and will not help the integration process. However, in my view, any person who is serving his local community is integrating through that very service. Indeed, the term *"community service"* is positive because it instils a belief that it is the duty of each person to serve their society and to help the members of the community. Accordingly, the German Government deserves praise rather than criticism for this policy.

Nevertheless, the responsibilities of a host government are not limited to arranging community service; rather, they should also guide the immigrants in a way that they are able to start contributing as quickly as possible to society. If the immigrants do not have the skills to enter the job market, they should be provided with some form of training or apprenticeships so that they can soon develop those skills. Any costs incurred in such training will be a valuable investment for the future of the nation.

In terms of security, if there is any doubt or suspicion raised about the character or backgrounds of certain immigrants, the authorities should be vigilant and monitor them until they are satisfied that they do not pose a risk to society. Some may consider this an intrusive policy, yet protecting society from danger and maintaining the peace and security of the nation are paramount objectives for any government. Certainly, if there are any immigrants who come with the intention of spreading mischief or creating disorder, they are directly contravening Islam's teachings. Indeed, chapter 2, verse 192 of the Holy Qur'an states that whilst murder is a truly heinous crime, to spread disorder and to provoke hatred is a crime of even greater magnitude. Of course, this does not mean that to kill someone is a small or insignificant crime; rather, it signifies that the ramifications of fuelling the flames of disorder in society are higher still. Ultimately, provocation and incitement can cause huge damage to a society and lead to conflicts and wars in which scores of innocent people are targeted or oppressed.

The Holy Prophet Muhammad[sa] also said that a true Muslim is he from whose tongue and hand all others are safe.[9]

How then, can it be said that Islam is a religion that promotes violence or radicalism? How can it be said that Islam spreads disorder in society? How can it be claimed that

Islam seeks to violate the honour of women? How can it be said that Islam permits its followers to usurp the property or wealth of others?

Anyone who is guilty of such crimes, whether they justify it in Islam's name or not, is far-removed from its teachings and will stand accountable for their atrocities. In every respect, Islam requires Muslims to display the highest standards of integrity and virtue. For example, in chapter 2, verse 189 of the Holy Qur'an, Allah the Almighty has admonished Muslims that they must never acquire wealth or property through means of deception; rather, Muslims are taught to be honest, trustworthy and to uphold the truth in all respects.

Similarly, in chapter 83, verses 2 to 4, Muslims are taught the importance of fair dealing in matters of business and trade. Allah the Almighty states:

"Woe unto those who give short measure. Those who, when they take by measure from other people, take it full. But when they give by measure to others or weigh to them, they give them less."

These verses state that those who are exploitative in business transactions, seeking unjust benefit for themselves at the expense of others, are those who are cursed and will ultimately be humiliated. The truth is that Islam has safeguarded society from all forms of cruelty and injustice and protects the life and property of every single person. It is therefore, a cause of deep regret and grief that people continue to make false allegations against the blessed character of the Holy Prophet Muhammad[sa], when he was the one who brought about a unique spiritual and moral revolution in society. Indeed, never in the history of humanity have such examples of moral integrity been seen as were displayed by the early Muslims. If his companions quarrelled, it was not to take advantage of each other; rather, it was to ensure that the rights of the other party were fulfilled.

For instance, once a companion of the Holy Prophet Muhammad[sa] came to the market to sell his horse for 200 dinars. When another companion of the Holy Prophet[sa] came forward to buy the horse, he told him that 200 dinars was far too low and that a fair price would be 500 dinars. He said that he did not wish to take charity and wanted to make a lawful and fair purchase and so, he would pay 500 dinars. Upon this, the Muslim seller said that he also did not wish to take charity and wished to make a fair sale and so, he only wanted 200 dinars.[10] Hence, their argument was for the sake of protecting the rights of the other person, in spite of the personal cost to themselves.

Imagine, if all members of society were able to live by and uphold such values. How magnificent a society would that be! A society in which every citizen prioritised honesty and strove for the common good. In other words, an Islamic society. If anyone wishes to know what Islam represents they should look at such noble examples, rather than those who sow division and intolerance falsely in its name. Certainly, today it is the need of the time that we all, Muslim or non-Muslim, pause and contemplate upon the consequences of our actions. With great pride, we speak of how the world has developed into an inter-connected global village and marvel at the speed of communication and travel.

Yet, alongside such advancement, we should realise that our responsibilities to the world have also increased. In terms of the migration crisis, wherever there are people subject to cruelties and brutalities in their home countries, it is up to the international community to help them. The priority should be to try to reconcile the peoples of those nations and to end wars, and to bring about sustainable peace; however, if that is not possible, it is our moral duty to open our hearts to those who are genuinely suffering.

Society should not reject genuine refugees who are suffering through no fault of their own. Society should not cast aside innocent people who only want the opportunity to live in peace, and who desire to be good citizens and follow the laws of the land in which they live. Instead, we should be there to give a helping hand to those whose lives have been broken, who have been tormented and who are utterly helpless, vulnerable and defenceless. Let us prove our humanity. Let us show our compassion. Let us be there to shoulder the burdens of those who are in desperate need.

On the other side, immigrants also have great responsibilities in their new countries. As I have said, they must seek to contribute to their new society and strive to integrate. They should not isolate themselves or cut themselves off from the local community, but should serve their adopted home and work towards its continued development and progress. Together, we must seek to find ways in which people of different backgrounds and heritages can live together harmoniously.

As I said, the world is now like a global village and so we are not living in those bygone eras where what happened in one country, only affected the local community or, at most, the neighbouring nations. Rather, we now live in a time where a disturbance or conflict in any country has ramifications and consequences for the rest of the world. Thus, instead of fearing one another, we should strive to solve problems through mutual dialogue and with a spirit of tolerance and compassion.

Our goal and objective should be nothing less than to establish peace in every village, town or city of every nation in the world.

The Ahmadiyya Muslim Community has always strived to fulfil this objective and to this end, we propagate what we consider to be the key ingredient to peace, which is a firm belief that we are all the creation of God Almighty and He created mankind so that they would recognise Him, and fulfil the rights of one another. We are certain that if mankind comes to this realisation, true and long-lasting peace can prevail.

Sadly, we are witnessing quite the opposite. Rather than coming together and seeking peace through the existence of God Almighty, mankind is embroiled in striving for peace through material means alone. Day by day, mankind is moving further away from religion and spirituality, and the results are terrifying. It is my firm conviction that belief in God Almighty is the only means of salvation and the only way to bring about true peace, both at a national and international level. And so, it is my deepest desire and ardent prayer, that the world comes to recognise its Creator and comes to follow His true teachings. Instead of pursuing personal or political objectives, I pray that today's leaders fulfil the rights of all people irrespective of caste, creed or colour.

With all my heart, I pray that the gulf that exists between mankind and God Almighty is eliminated and that we come to see with our own eyes true peace prevail throughout the world. I thank you all very much.

" The Holy Prophet of Islam[sa] said that the giving hand is far greater than the one that takes. On many occasions people sought to help his companions, but they refused to accept and preferred to earn a living for themselves.

— His Holiness Mirza Masroor Ahmad,
Khalifatul-Masih V[aba]

True *and* Sustainable World Peace

16TH NATIONAL PEACE SYMPOSIUM
The Baitul Futuh Mosque, London, UK
9 MARCH 2019

"The most quickly rewarded good deeds are kindness and upholding the ties of kinship, and the most quickly punished evil deeds are injustice and severing the ties of kinship."

— The Holy Prophet Muhammad[sa]

True *and* Sustainable World Peace

Bismillahir Rahmanir Raheem, in the Name of Allah, the Gracious, Ever Merciful. All distinguished guests, *Assalamo Alaikum Wa Rahmatullahe Wa Barakatohu* – peace and blessings of Allah be upon you all.

Each year, the Ahmadiyya Muslim Community hosts this Peace Symposium, in which current issues and the overall state of the world are analysed and, in my address, I seek to present answers to these contemporary issues in light of the teachings of Islam. In terms of what impact this event has on the wider world, I have said before that I do not know. However, regardless of its effect, we shall never give up our efforts to promote peace and justice, and certainly, I am sure all of you share our ardent desire for true and long-lasting peace to be established in the world.

Indeed, I am sure all of you hope to see an end to the many conflicts and wars that have blighted the world in recent times, and for a peaceful world to emerge in which all people and all nations live amicably, and fulfil the rights of one another. Yet, the tragic and devastating truth is that each year, instead of pulling back from war and conflict, the opposite is proving true. Rivalries are intensifying, new battle lines are being drawn, whilst existing hostilities show little sign of abating.

Though we are all aware that we are passing through difficult times, most people do not realise the extent to which the relations between certain nations have deteriorated and how potentially disastrous the consequences could prove to be. For example, in a recent column published by Bloomberg Businessweek, the journalist Peter Coy writes:

> *"Nuclear war gets surprisingly little attention considering there are enough nukes to end human civilisation in hours... The reason to pay attention is that arms control – especially between the U.S. and Russia – has broken down. A fresh nuclear arms race appears to be taking shape. As for what anyone can do: arms control moves forward in response to public pressure, when humanity speaks louder than arms merchants and bellicose world leaders."* [1]

In his article, he also quotes a senior fellow of the Middlebury Institute of International Studies, Nikolai Sokov, who warns:

"All signs point in the direction of a serious combined nuclear-conventional arms race in Europe." [2]

The rest of the article reinforces the point that another global arms race has begun and that the threat of nuclear war should not be underestimated. In recent days, the world witnessed a sudden escalation and tension between India and Pakistan. Both countries are nuclear powers and both have built alliances with other nations, whether openly or in secret, which means that the potential consequences of a war would be extensive and far-reaching.

I have expressed my view on many occasions that the leaders of some of the nuclear powers are trigger-happy and appear not to appreciate the truly grave consequences of nuclear warfare.[3] Not only do such weapons have the power to annihilate the countries targeted, but also have the potential to destroy the peace and stability of the entire world. Thus, it is imperative that nations and their leaders do not focus only on their own national interests, but consider what is best for the world at large. Dialogue with other nations and communities is vital, and each party should work together with a spirit of tolerance and with the shared objective of developing true and sustainable peace in the world.

In a recent interview with Spiegel Online, the former Foreign Minister of Germany, Sigmar Gabriel, has warned of underestimating the dangers posed by the current geopolitical situation and he compares the current political state to the circumstances of the world in 1945 and 1989. The former German Foreign Minister said:

"The world is changing dramatically…the old West has broken apart…It is a drastic change from the past 70 years, when we could depend on the U.S. as a leading nation. We are going through a fight for European sovereignty in a completely changed world." [4]

Similarly, in a New York Times article, the former leader of the Soviet Union, Mikhail Gorbachev writes that following the recent suspension of the I.N.F. Treaty by the United States and Russia, a new nuclear arms race has begun. Mr Gorbachev writes:

"A new arms race has been announced. The I.N.F. Treaty is not the first victim of the militarization of world affairs. In 2002, the United States withdrew from the Antiballistic Missile Treaty; this year, from the Iran nuclear deal. Military expenditures have soared to astronomical levels and keep rising." [5]

Warning about the risk of a nuclear war, Mr Gorbachev writes:

"There will be no winner in a 'war of all against all' — particularly if it ends in a nuclear war. And that is a possibility that cannot be ruled out. An unrelenting arms race, international tensions, hostility and universal mistrust will only increase the risk." [6]

Hence, expert commentators and experienced politicians are reaching the conclusion that nuclear war no longer remains a remote and distant prospect, but is a growing threat that can no longer be discounted.

If we glance at just a few of today's pressing issues, it is clear that the world is heading in an ominous direction. During the past year, the United States claimed with a degree of confidence, that it was close to securing a historic peace deal with North Korea, but in recent days, it has become clear that nothing of substance has been achieved.

Conflict in the Middle East continues to rage. Over almost a decade, Syria has been ravaged by bloodshed and torn asunder. It is said that the civil war is now edging towards an end, but what has the past decade achieved except the death of hundreds of thousands of innocent people and the displacement of millions of others? Nothing positive has emerged and the future remains uncertain and precarious, as tensions rise between nations who have their own vested interests tied into the future of Syria.

On one side, Russia and Turkey are aligning, whilst on the other side, the United States and Saudi Arabia are joining together and are ratcheting up pressure on Iran and seeking further sanctions against them. Political experts are openly expressing that the objective of these nations is to dominate the Middle East. Another flashpoint and source of conflict are the worsening relations between Turkey and the Kurdish groups who seek autonomy.

Thus, the world is stuck in a vicious cycle of conflict and counter-conflict, as rivalries ferment and hatreds become ever more deeply entrenched. No one knows where such issues will finally lead us or how horrific the consequences will prove to be. What I have mentioned is just the tip of the iceberg. There are many other issues of concern that threaten the peace and well-being of the world.

For example, it is said that the terrorist group Daesh is on the verge of collapse and that their so-called Khilafat is finished. Yet, experts also warn that though Daesh has lost its territory, its hateful ideology persists and its members who have survived are now scattering and could eventually regroup and perpetrate attacks in Europe or elsewhere.

Furthermore, nationalism has reared its ugly head again and far-right parties are gaining popularity across the Western world. They may not have secured outright political majorities, but unless justice at all levels of society prevails, they will continue to gain support. One of the core reasons underpinning their popularity has been widespread immigration, which has caused resentment and a belief that existing indigenous citizens are being short-changed in order to fund and support immigrants. I have spoken on this issue at length in the past and so I do not need to go over old ground. Suffice to say, that if genuine efforts are made to cultivate peace and to help all countries achieve their potential, the desperation of people to flee their homes would automatically subside.

All that most people desire is the ability to provide for their families and it is only when such opportunities are denied to them that they seek to leave their homes in search of a better life. Accordingly, the long-term solution to the immigration crisis has to be to establish peace in war-torn countries and to help the local people, who have been forced to endure lives of misery and danger, to live peacefully.

In the short term, where refugees or asylum seekers come to the West due to the prevailing political or religious conditions in their own countries, they should be treated with dignity and respect. At the same time, whatever support they are given should not be at the expense of existing citizens.

Immigrants should be strongly encouraged to enter employment as soon as possible, rather than living off benefits for long periods. They should work hard, seek to stand upon their own two feet and contribute positively to their new society. Otherwise, if they are continually funded by taxpayers' money, it will inevitably lead to grievances. Indeed, it is my belief that the underlying cause of most resentment in society tends to be economic and financial frustration. Certain groups take advantage of such anxiety by laying the blame at the feet of immigrants or at the followers of religion and incite sentiments of hatred towards them.

Thus, an impression has developed in Europe that Asians, Africans and particularly Muslim immigrants are a threat to society. In the United States, there are similar fears regarding Muslims and also Hispanics seeking to enter the country through Mexico. Nonetheless, I firmly believe that if the major powers set aside their own vested interests and strive earnestly towards improving the economic conditions of poorer nations and treat them with sympathy and respect, such issues would never arise.

Here in the United Kingdom, there is currently a great deal of uncertainty regarding Brexit and the UK's future relationship with the European Union. I made my own views on this topic clear during an address at the European Parliament in 2012. Whilst addressing, I said:

"You should make all possible efforts to preserve this unity by honouring each other's rights. The fears and worries held by members of the general public must be removed." [7]

I also said:

> *"Remember that the strength of Europe lies in its remaining united and together as one. Such unity will not only benefit you here in Europe, but at a global level will be the means for this continent to maintain its strength and influence."* [8]

In my speech seven years ago, I focused upon the importance of removing the fears of the public about immigration and emphasising the benefits of unity.

However, people's concerns were not adequately addressed and so increasingly, people across Europe have come to question the benefits of the European Union. The starkest example is, of course, Brexit but in many European countries, such as Italy and Spain, and even Germany, far-right or nationalist parties are gaining popularity and winning seats at the political table through which they are striving to further weaken the European Union, and pursuing an anti-immigrant agenda.

Hence, where I had hoped for greater unity in Europe, the past few years have witnessed increased division and turmoil. Why have such frustrations come to the fore? They are derived from economic difficulties and a failure of governments to act with justice and to protect the rights of their citizens. My own view remains that international co-operation is a positive and unifying force for good. Thus, at the European Parliament, I also said:

> *"From an Islamic perspective, we should strive for the entire world to unite together. In terms of currency, the world should be united...In terms of free business and trade, the world should be united and in terms of freedom of movement and immigration, cohesive and practical policies should be developed, so that the world can become united."* [9]

Consequently, the Islamic viewpoint is that peace can best be achieved through unity. Yet, regretfully, instead of uniting, we are seeking separation and prioritising our individual interests over the collective interests of the world. I believe that such policies will, and already are, undermining the world's peace and security. According to Islam, for peace to prevail, justice between nations is a prerequisite.

Where countries face difficulties, other nations should seek to help them selflessly, without pushing their own agendas. For example, the Holy Qur'an states that if there is a war or conflict between two parties, other nations should mediate impartially and seek to bring about a peaceful settlement. However, if one side continues to be unjust and does not move towards a peaceful outcome, then the other nations should unite together to stop the aggressor. Once the aggressive nations or party refrains from wrongdoing, Islam categorically instructs that revenge should not be sought through unjust sanctions or by plundering their resources.[10]

However, time and again, we have seen examples of countries that have intervened in war-torn nations or given aid to deprived countries on the pretext of bringing peace, but have attached strings that enable them to take control of the weaker country's resources. Rather than being content with their own wealth, powerful countries seek to assert their control over weaker nations.

As I have said, the root cause of frustration and the resulting hostility, whether in the East or the West, is economic injustice and so, it is essential that a concerted effort is made to bridge the economic divide amongst nations and their people. Furthermore, we must unite in our efforts to end all forms of extremism and prejudice, whether religious, racial or of any other kind.

Where it is clear that people are suffering and that their leaders are not protecting their rights, those international organisations founded for the sake of preserving the peace of the world, notably the United Nations, should exercise lawful and proportionate pressure in order to defend the rights of law-abiding citizens and to push for peace and justice.

In terms of Islam, you may wonder what it can teach us about bringing peace in the world when much of the instability and conflict in recent years has centred around Muslim countries. Yet the sorry state of those nations is because they have moved far away from the true teachings of Islam.

To get an accurate portrayal of Islamic governance and leadership we should look to the era of the Founder of Islam, the Holy Prophet Muhammad[sa]. After the Holy Prophet[sa] migrated to the city of Madinah, he formed a covenant with the Jewish people, whereby the Muslims and the Jewish citizens were to live together peacefully and with a spirit of mutual sympathy, tolerance and equity.

The covenant proved to be a magnificent charter of human rights and governance, and ensured peace between the different communities living in Madinah. According to its terms, all people, regardless of their faith or ethnicity, were bound to respect the rights of one another. Freedom of belief and freedom of conscience were cornerstones of that treaty.

Unity underpinned the agreement, whereby if Madinah was attacked or threatened, the Muslims and Jews would join forces to defend it together and as one. Further, each community had the right to solve their internal issues according to their respective beliefs and customs. History testifies to the fact that the Holy Prophet of Islam[sa] upheld every aspect of that agreement.

As immigrants, the Muslims sought to serve their new society and to respect the rights of all the citizens of Madinah. It was an outstanding example of successful integration and a manifestation of a peaceful and tolerant multicultural society. The Treaty of Madinah was based directly upon the teachings of the Holy Qur'an. For example, chapter 16, verse 91 of the Holy Qur'an states:

"Verily, Allah enjoins justice, and the doing of good to others; and giving like kindred…"

Thus, the Holy Qur'an has outlined three levels of engagement with other people and other communities. The first and minimum level is of justice, whereby the Holy Qur'an advocates the need to treat everyone fairly and equitably. The standards of justice required by Islam are outlined in chapter 4, verse 136 of the Holy Qur'an, which states:

"O ye who believe! Be strict in observing justice, and be witnesses for Allah, even though it be against yourselves or against parents and kindred. Whether he be rich or poor, Allah is more regardful of them both than you are. Therefore, follow not low desires so that you may be able to act equitably. And if you conceal the truth or evade it, then remember that Allah is well aware of what you do."

Hence, according to the Qur'an, justice requires that a person is willing to testify even against himself and his most loved ones in order to guard and protect the truth.

The second level of engagement advocated by the Holy Qur'an is that a person should not only be just, but should go beyond it by doing *"good to others"* by manifesting generosity and forgiveness. As I have already mentioned, the Holy Qur'an teaches that once you have successfully stopped an aggressive nation from inflicting further cruelties, you should not seek revenge or impose hardship upon it. Rather, you should seek to help them build up their economy and infrastructure. Where this will help them, it will also help you in the long term. If those countries, who have been centres of war or division, are enabled to prosper economically, they will no longer harbour frustrations or bear hatred for other countries. Nor will their people be forced to migrate. This is the wisdom underpinning the Islamic teaching of going beyond basic justice and exhibiting kindness and compassion.

The third level of engagement taught by the Holy Qur'an is to treat others in the same way that a mother treats her child, which is the most selfless form of love, as it is rendered without any expectations of reward. To treat others with this benevolent spirit is not easy, but this should be our constant aspiration.

Ultimately, to bring about peace, whether in Muslim nations or at a broader international level, it is necessary that at the very minimum, the demands of justice are fulfilled by governments so that all people are given their due rights and that selfish vested interests give way to what is fair and right.

Furthermore, international institutions, such as the United Nations, should treat each country equally, rather than bend to the will of certain powers. This is the means of peace. This is the road map to a better world. This is the only way we can prevent mankind from sliding further towards grave peril.

With these few words, it is my heartfelt prayer that may Allah the Almighty enable true peace to emerge and may the long shadows of war and conflict that hover above us be replaced by blue skies of peace and prosperity. I pray for an end to the frustrations and deprivation that have plagued the lives of countless people and have fuelled devastating wars and grievances across the world.

Instead of seeking to dominate others and assert their own rights, I pray that nations and their leaders come to see the benefit of fulfilling the rights of one another. Instead of laying the blame for the world's problems on certain religions or people of particular ethnicities, I pray that we show tolerance of each other's beliefs and customs, and value the diversity within our societies.

I pray that we come to see the best in humanity and use each other's strengths and skills to build a better world for our children and to cultivate lasting peace in society. Surely, the alternatives do not bear thinking about. Earlier, I quoted several experts who have warned of nuclear warfare and of a spiralling global arms race. Those articles, and many others, give weight to the belief that the world is hurtling towards a titanic catastrophe, the like of which mankind has never seen before and one that will be impossible to contain.

According to some estimates, the effects of a nuclear war could reach 90% of the world. Furthermore, if there is a nuclear war, we will not only be destroying the world today, but we will also be leaving behind a lasting trail of destruction and misery for our future generations. Hence, we must pause and reflect on the consequences of our actions.

We should not consider any issue or conflict, whether within a country or at an international level, to be insignificant. Whether we are dealing with economic issues or immigration, or any other crisis, we must show tolerance and strive to break down the barriers that divide us. We should utilise all of our energies and faculties to pursue peace by seeking to end every conflict amicably, through dialogue, and mutual compromise and by fulfilling the rights of one another.

May Allah the Almighty enable us to do so – Ameen. With these words, I would like to thank all of our guests for joining us here this evening. Thank you very much.

Pictures *of the* True Jihad

PHOTOGRAPHS FROM THE ADDRESSES OF
HIS HOLINESS MIRZA MASROOR AHMAD[ABA]
Britain | Germany | France

" As the Head of a worldwide Muslim community, it is my duty that I should draw the attention of the world towards establishing peace. I consider this my obligation because Islam's very meaning is peace and security.

— His Holiness Mirza Masroor Ahmad, Khalifatul-Masih V[aba]

▲ Press conference at the Baitul Futuh Mosque prior to the keynote address at the Peace Symposium 2016. Members of Parliament, Lords and senior political leaders attend the annual Symposium that takes place at the largest mosque in Western Europe.

His Holiness Mirza Masroor Ahmad – Khalifatul-Masih V[abs], is the head of the worldwide Ahmadiyya Muslim Community. He is at the heart of a global campaign for peace. In the photo above he delivers the keynote address that is broadcast across the world. In the photo below he leads a silent prayer following the address – people of all faiths and beliefs join him. (2016)

▲ His Holiness is a passionate advocate for universal human rights, justice and peace. Delivering addresses at parliaments across the world including Capitol Hill, the European Parliament and the House of Commons, he regularly meets presidents, prime ministers, heads of state, parliamentarians and ambassadors promoting dialogue and understanding whilst spreading the true and peaceful teachings of Islam. (Peace Symposium 2016)

▼ Below: Peace Symposium 2016, UK. Bottom right: Peace Symposium 2019. His Holiness' analysis of geopolitical conflicts and their resolution is based upon the Holy Qur'an and precedents established by the practice of the Founder of Islam: the Holy Prophet Muhammad, peace and blessings of Allah be upon him.

▲ His Holiness is internationally respected having spoken on a host of topics including religion and politics. The photo above is from the Peace Symposium 2019 in which several media outlets asked about the Islamic perspective on contemporary debates.

▲ In the keynote address delivered at the Ahmadiyya Muslim Research Association Conference, His Holiness urged Ahmadi Muslim academics to dedicate their lives in service to mankind. (2019)

His Holiness has consistently been warning that failure to establish peace could increase the number of conflicts, especially with the polarisation of societies around the world. He has been tireless in his efforts to promote peace, social justice and inter-faith dialogue. (Peace Symposium 2019)

▼ The words of His Holiness are a source of inspiration for millions around the world. After His Holiness' address at the Ahmadiyya Muslim Research Association Conference, the atmosphere was filled with excitement as if a new spirit had been breathed into researchers. (2019)

ISLAM & EUROPA
Ein Kampf der Kulturen?

BERLIN, 22. OKTOBER 2019

In the address delivered in Berlin, His Holiness discussed the question of Islam being compatible with the West. He explained that there is no need to fear true Islam as the Holy Qur'an places great emphasis on discharging the rights of others, and being loyal to one's country of residence. (2019)

▲ His Holiness speaks at UNESCO, Paris. His keynote address discussed education, the Islamic importance stressed upon it and the contribution of Muslims in advancing science. (2019)

▼ The Tahir Hall in the Baitul Futuh Mosque is filled to maximum capacity at the Peace Symposium every year, as people from all around the world gather to listen to the Islamic solution on how to establish peace in the current climate. (2019)

▼ In his keynote address delivered in Berlin, three decades after the famous symbol of division, the Berlin Wall, was knocked down, His Holiness urged today's leaders and governments to demolish the walls of hatred and conflict that have plagued modern-day society. (2019)

▲ The address delivered in Berlin was titled *Islam & Europe: A Clash of Civilisations?* His Holiness spoke on the rise of immigration to Europe and the subsequent fears and anxieties that have arisen as a result. He spoke about the duties and roles of immigrants, emphasising that they should contribute to the country that granted them refuge. He also outlined the responsibility of host nations to help immigrants re-build their lives. (2019)

Two panoramic photos of addresses in two different countries. Top: His Holiness Mirza Masroor Ahmad[aba] delivers an address at the Jalsa Salana (Annual Convention) of the Ahmadiyya Muslim Community in Germany. (2018)

Below: a photo from the Peace Symposium 2019, UK. Mayors, representatives of the British Armed Forces and members of parliament from around the world attend the Peace Symposium each year.

▲ In the UNESCO address His Holiness explained that the core principles of Islam revolve around humanitarian acts. His address demonstrated the vast nature of Islamic teachings that not only educate on how to establish geopolitical peace, but also encourage Muslims to make advancements in education and the attainment of knowledge. (2019)

▼ In his keynote address at the Ahmadiyya Muslim Research Association Conference, His Holiness explained the reasons for the decline in academic prestige on the part of Muslims; describing what is required for the re-emergence of the Islamic Golden Age. (2019)

Islamic Principles *on* Education *and* Serving Humanity

UNESCO HEADQUARTERS
Paris, France
8 OCTOBER 2019

"If anyone travels on a road in search of knowledge, Allah will cause him to travel on one of the roads of Paradise."

— The Holy Prophet Muhammad[sa]

Islamic Principles *on* Education *and* Serving Humanity

Bismillahir Rahmanir Raheem – in the Name of Allah, the Gracious, Ever Merciful. All distinguished guests, *Assalamo Alaikum Wa Rahmatullahe Wa Barakatohu* – peace and blessings of Allah be upon you all.

First of all, I would like to take this opportunity to thank the UNESCO administration for graciously permitting us to hold this event today.

I would also like to place on record my sincere gratitude to all the guests who have accepted our invitation and have come to listen to a person, who is neither a politician, nor a political leader nor a scientist, but rather is the head of a religious community – the Ahmadiyya Muslim Community.

The founding objectives of UNESCO are excellent and

praiseworthy. Amongst its objectives are fostering peace and respect, promoting the rule of law, human rights and education across the world. UNESCO also advocates for press freedom and protecting different cultures and heritages. Another of its stated goals is to eradicate poverty, to promote sustainable global growth and development, and to try to ensure that humanity leaves behind a positive legacy, from which future generations can benefit.

You may be surprised to learn that Islamic teachings require Muslims to work towards fulfilling these same objectives and to continually strive for the progress of humanity. Such service is based upon the very first chapter of the Holy Qur'an, which states that Allah the Almighty is the *"Lord of all the worlds"*.[1]

This verse is central to the Islamic faith, whereby Muslims are taught that God Almighty is not just their Lord and Provider, but He is the Provider and Sustainer of all humankind. He is the Gracious and Merciful and so, irrespective of caste, creed or colour, God Almighty fulfils the needs of His creation. Given this, true Muslims firmly believe that all humans are born equal and that regardless of differences of belief, the values of mutual respect and tolerance must be firmly embedded within society.

A beautiful Islamic principle given in chapter 2, verse 139 of the Holy Qur'an, is that Muslims should seek to follow the ways of Allah the Almighty and adopt His attributes.

As mentioned, Allah's Grace is all-encompassing and He is the Provider and Sustainer for all people, including those who deny His existence. His Grace and Mercy remains even with those who continually speak ill of Him or who conduct cruelties in the world.

In Islam, the philosophy of punishment or sanction established by God Almighty is weighted more towards the hereafter, whilst in this life, Allah the Almighty continues to manifest His Grace and Mercy upon the world. By instructing Muslims to adopt His ways, Allah the Almighty has instructed them to show compassion and sympathy to their fellow creation. In light of this, it is a religious obligation on Muslims to fulfil the requirements of other people, irrespective of religion, culture or ethnicity and to always be kind and empathetic to the emotions and needs of others.

Moreover, the Holy Qur'an has pronounced that the Holy Prophet of Islam (peace and blessings of Allah be upon him) was sent to the world by God Almighty as a source of unparalleled mercy and benevolence for all humanity.[2] He was the practical manifestation of the compassionate teachings of Islam. After he founded Islam, the Holy Prophet Muhammad (peace and blessings of Allah be upon him) and his followers were subjected to brutal and inhumane treatment by the non-Muslims of Makkah, which they endured with patience and restraint.

Finally, after suffering years of relentless persecution, they migrated to the city of Madinah where the Holy Prophet Muhammad (peace and blessings of Allah be upon him) formed a covenant of peace between the Muslim migrants, the Jewish people and other members of society. According to its terms, the divergent groups pledged to live peacefully, to fulfil the rights of one another and to foster a spirit of mutual sympathy, tolerance and cooperation.

The Holy Prophet Muhammad (peace and blessings of Allah be upon him) was elected as the head of state and under his leadership, the covenant proved to be a magnificent charter of human rights and governance, and it ensured peace between the different communities. The Prophet of Islam (peace and blessings of Allah be upon him) established an impartial judiciary for dispute resolution. He made it clear that there would be one law for the rich and powerful and for the poor and weak, and all people would be treated equally according to the law of the land.

For example, on one occasion, an affluent lady committed a crime and many people suggested that, given her high standing in society, it was better to turn a blind eye to her crimes. The Holy Prophet Muhammad (peace and blessings of Allah be upon him) rejected their advice and made it clear that even if his daughter committed an offence, she too would be subject to the law and no favouritism or nepotism would occur.[3]

In addition, the Prophet of Islam (peace and blessings of Allah be upon him) established an excellent education system, through which the intellectual standards of that society were raised. Literate and well-educated people were instructed to teach the illiterate. Special measures were put in place to provide education to orphans and other vulnerable members of society. This was all done so that the weak and powerless could stand on their own two feet and advance.

A taxation system was established, whereby taxes were levied on wealthier members of society and the proceeds were used to provide financial aid for disadvantaged members of society. According to the teachings of the Holy Qur'an, the Prophet of Islam (peace and blessings of Allah be upon him) established a code of business and financial ethics to ensure that trading was fair and honest.

In an age when slavery was rampant and slave-owners treated their slaves mercilessly, the Prophet of Islam (peace and blessings of Allah be upon him) sought to bring about a revolution in society. Slave-owners were ordered to treat their slaves with compassion and respect, and the Holy Prophet Muhammad (peace and blessings of Allah be upon him) repeatedly urged them to free them.[4]

Also, under the leadership of the Holy Prophet Muhammad (peace and blessings of Allah be upon him), a system of public sanitation was developed. A city cleaning programme was implemented and people were educated about the importance of personal hygiene and physical health. The roads of the city were expanded and improved. A census was conducted to collect data and to identify the needs of the citizens.

Thus, during the 7th century, under the government led by the Prophet of Islam (peace and blessings of Allah be upon him), astonishing progress was made in Madinah to advance the cause of individual and collective rights. Indeed, for the very first time amongst the Arabs, an orderly and civilised society was established.

In many ways, it was a model society, in terms of infrastructure, services and more importantly, in terms of the unity and tolerance displayed in what was a multicultural society. The Muslims were immigrants, yet they integrated smoothly into the local society and contributed to its success and development.

Moving on, in terms of the teachings of Islam, it is a cause of profound sadness that in today's world, the Holy Prophet of Islam (peace and blessings of Allah be upon him) has been grievously mischaracterised. He has been branded as a belligerent leader, when nothing could be further from the truth.

The reality is that the Prophet of Islam (peace and blessings of Allah be upon him) spent every moment of his life championing the rights of all people and through the teachings of Islam, he established an incomparable and timeless charter of human rights. For example, he taught that people should respect the beliefs and feelings of one another. They should abstain from criticising what others held sacred.

Once, a Jewish person came to him and complained about the conduct of one of his closest companion. The Prophet of Islam (peace and blessings of Allah be upon him) summoned him and asked what had transpired. He said that the Jew had claimed that Moses (peace be upon him) was superior in rank to the Prophet of Islam (peace and blessings of Allah be upon him) and he could not tolerate this. He had strongly refuted it and said that the Holy Prophet of Islam (peace and blessings of Allah be upon him) was of a higher rank. Upon this, the Holy Prophet Muhammad (peace and blessings of Allah be upon him) expressed his displeasure with his closest confidant and said that he should not have argued with the Jew, and should instead have respected his religious sentiments.[5]

These were his peerless teachings and in my view, it is deeply regrettable that the principle of mutual respect, which is the means of establishing love and unity, has been sacrificed in the modern world in the name of so-called freedom and even in the name of entertainment.

Even the founders of religion are no longer spared mockery and contempt, even though their derision causes anguish and pain to millions of their followers around the world. On the other hand, the Holy Qur'an goes as far as saying that Muslims should not even speak ill of the idols of others, because it will cause them distress and in turn, they may speak ill of God Almighty and consequently, the peace and unity of society would suffer.[6]

In terms of fulfilling the rights of the weak and poor, the Holy Prophet of Islam (peace and blessings of Allah be upon him) established various schemes and projects to raise their standards of living and to ensure that they were not deprived of their dignity. He said that whilst most people afforded a high status to those who were wealthy and powerful, a poor person who was moral and considerate had far greater value than a rich person who cared not for the feelings of others, and merely lived off his name.

Even in small matters, the Holy Prophet of Islam (peace and blessings of Allah be upon him) paid great attention to ensuring that the feelings of underprivileged people were protected. For example, he instructed Muslims to always invite the poor and needy to their dinner parties or social gatherings. If less affluent people were exploited by the rich or powerful, the Prophet of Islam (peace and blessings of Allah be upon him) instructed his followers to help the weaker party attain justice.

The Holy Prophet (peace and blessings of Allah be upon him) always sought to eliminate slavery. In this regard, to his own followers, the Prophet of Islam (peace and blessings of Allah be upon him) repeatedly advocated the freeing of slaves and instructed that if it was not immediately possible for them to release them, then at the very minimum, they were to feed and clothe them, in the same way they fed and clothed themselves.[7]

Another issue often raised is of women's rights and it is often alleged that Islam denies women's rights. Nothing could be further from the truth! Rather, Islam established the rights of women and girls for the first time. At a time when women and girls were discriminated against and often looked down upon, the Holy Prophet of Islam (peace and blessings of Allah be upon him) instructed his followers to ensure that girls were educated and respected.

Indeed, he said that if a person had three daughters, whom they educated and guided in the best way, they would be sure to enter paradise.[8] This is contrary to the extremist's claim that a violent Jihad and the slaughter of non-Muslims will take a person to heaven. The Prophet of Islam (peace and blessings of Allah be upon him) taught that the way to enter heaven was by educating and instilling moral values within girls.

Based upon these teachings, Ahmadi Muslim girls across the world are educated and are excelling in various fields. They are becoming doctors, teachers and architects and entering other professions through which they can serve humanity. We ensure that girls are given equal access to education as boys. Hence, the literacy rate of Ahmadi Muslim girls in the developing world is at least 99%. Besides education, Islam was the religion that first gave women the right to inheritance, the right to divorce and many other human rights.

Furthermore, the Holy Prophet (peace and blessings of Allah be upon him) emphasised the rights of one's neighbours and said that Allah the Almighty had placed such great emphasis upon their rights, that he came to think that neighbours would be classed amongst a person's rightful heirs.[9] Thus, the Prophet of Islam (peace and blessings of Allah be upon him) established universal human rights that were due to each individual, irrespective of their beliefs, social status or ethnicity.

I have just spoken about how the Holy Prophet of Islam (peace and blessings of Allah be upon him) focused a great deal on the importance of education. This was reflected in the aftermath of the first battle in the history of Islam. Despite being extremely ill-equipped they were able to defeat the much stronger Makkan army with the help of Allah the Almighty.

Thereafter, the Holy Prophet Muhammad (peace and blessings of Allah be upon him) offered to release those prisoners of war who were literate, on condition they first taught illiterate members of society how to read and write. In this way, many centuries ago, the Prophet of Islam (peace and blessings of Allah be upon him) established a very successful model for the rehabilitation and re-integration into society of prisoners, which benefited society at large.

It is often alleged that Islam is a religion of violence or warfare but the truth is, and is stated in the Holy Qur'an, that permission to fight back was granted to establish and preserve the principles of freedom of belief and freedom of conscience for all mankind. The Qur'an states that if the Muslims did not defend themselves against the Makkan army then no church, synagogue, temple, mosque or any other place of worship would be safe, because the opponents of Islam were determined to eliminate all forms of religion.[10]

In reality, if the early Muslims engaged in warfare it was always defensive and fought for the sake of establishing long-term peace, and to protect the right of all people to live with freedom.

If today there are Muslims who have adopted extremist tactics or who preach violence, it is because they have abandoned Islam's teachings or are wholly ignorant of it. Where individuals or groups conduct terrorism, it is to gain power or to enrich themselves. Similarly, where countries adopt unjust and extreme policies, their goals are invariably linked to gaining geopolitical benefit and asserting their dominance over others. Their conduct has nothing to do with Islam.

The Holy Qur'an states very clearly that there should be

no compulsion in matters of faith. Islam prohibits Muslims from aggression and so the Prophet of Islam (peace and blessings of Allah be upon him) and his four rightly guided Caliphs never sought war or violence, and, at all times, sought peace and reconciliation and made countless sacrifices in its cause.

Another allegation levelled against Islam by certain critics is that it is a backward and archaic religion or one that does not promote intellectual advancement. This is a lazy stereotype that is based on fiction rather than fact. It is a baseless allegation. The Holy Qur'an itself has signified the importance of education by teaching the prayer: *"O my Lord, increase me in knowledge".*[11]

Where this prayer is a source of great help to Muslims, it also inspires them towards learning and advancing the cause of human knowledge.

The truth is that the Holy Qur'an and the teachings of the Holy Prophet of Islam (peace and blessings of Allah be upon him) inspired the works of generations of Muslim intellectuals, philosophers and inventors in the Middle Ages. Indeed, if we look back more than a millennium, we see how Muslim scientists and inventors played a fundamental role in advancing knowledge and developing technologies, which transformed the world and remain in use today.

For example, the first ever camera was developed by Ibn Haytham and his revolutionary work was recognised by UNESCO, when he was declared as a *"pioneer of modern optics"*. It is also interesting to note that the word camera is derived from the Arabic word *"qamara"*.

In the 12th century, a Muslim cartographer produced what was regarded as the most extensive and accurate world map of the medieval times, which was used for centuries by travellers.

Furthermore, in the field of medicine, many Muslim physicians and scientists made great discoveries and pioneered many inventions that remain in use today. Many of the surgical instruments were pioneered by the Muslim physician Al-Zahrawi in the 10th century.

In the 17th century, an English physician, William Harvey famously carried out what was considered as ground-breaking research regarding blood circulation and the functioning of the heart. However, it was later discovered that more than 400 years before Harvey's research, Ibn Nafees, an Arab physician, had already detailed the basics of pulmonary circulation in an Arabic textbook.

In the 9th century, Jabir ibn Hayyan brought about a revolution in the field of chemistry. He invented many of the basic processes and apparatus still in use today.

The principles of Algebra were first developed by a Muslim, as was much of the theory of Trigonometry.

In the modern world, algorithms are the basis of modern computing technology and they too were first developed by

Muslims.

The contribution of Muslims to intellectual enlightenment is still recognised. For example, a New York Times article, published by their science reporter, Dennis Overbye, mentions the role of the Muslim polymath Al-Tusi. The author states:

> *"Al-Tusi thrived there, publishing many great works on astronomy, ethics, mathematics and philosophy, that marked him as one of the great intellectuals of his age…Muslims created a society that in the Middle Ages was the scientific centre of the world. The Arabic language was synonymous with learning and science for 500 years, a golden age that can count among its credits the precursors to modern universities…"* [12]

Hence, from the outset, Islam emphasised the immense value of learning and pushing the boundaries of human knowledge.

Since it was founded in 1889, the Ahmadiyya Muslim Community has always promoted education amongst its members. With the Grace of Allah, the very first Muslim Nobel Laureate was an Ahmadi Muslim, Professor Dr Abdus Salam, an eminent physicist who won the Nobel Prize for Physics in 1979. Throughout his life, Professor Salam spoke of how Islam, and the Holy Qur'an in particular, was the inspiration and guiding light behind his work. In fact, he used to say that there were around 750 verses in the Holy Qur'an directly related to science which enhanced our understanding of nature and the universe.

Furthermore, the Third Caliph of our Community desired for a new dawn of great Muslim scientists and academics to emerge and so, within our Community, he started a tradition of awarding gold medals for academic excellence. Each year, hundreds of Ahmadi Muslim boys and girls, or men and women, are awarded gold medals.

Certainly, we believe that access to education is key to breaking the cycle of poverty that has plagued economically weak countries for generations. We learn this from the Holy Prophet of Islam (peace and blessings of Allah be upon him) who urged Muslims to fund the education of vulnerable members of society, such as orphans.

He taught that spiritual advancement was intrinsically linked to serving humanity and so, a Muslim could not attain the love of God Almighty just through worship and prayer, rather the love of God Almighty required Muslims to serve humanity. Thus, in chapter 90, verses 15 to 17 of the Holy Qur'an, Muslims are instructed to work to eradicate hunger and poverty, to fulfil the needs of orphans and to educate vulnerable and poor children, so that opportunities open up for them to develop.

In all parts of the world, the Ahmadiyya Muslim Community acts upon these noble teachings to the best of its abilities. We believe that Islam is a religion of love and compassion and so, we serve humanity without making any distinction based on the religion or ethnicity of those who we help.

Therefore, in remote and poverty-stricken parts of Africa, we have established primary and secondary schools and we have also opened hospitals and clinics. We are providing clean running water in remote villages, which mean that children are free to go to school, instead of spending their days travelling for miles seeking to collect pond-water for their domestic family use.

We have also set up a project of building model villages, which include community halls, access to clean water, solar energy infrastructure and various other facilities. All of these services are provided to the local people, irrespective of their background or beliefs and are motivated entirely by our religion.

Where, out of human sympathy, we seek to eradicate poverty and destitution, we also consider it to be the key to developing sustainable peace in the world. Only if people have food to eat, water to drink, shelter, schooling for their children and healthcare will they be able to live in peace and escape the deadly clutches of frustration and resentment that lead people towards extremism.

These are all basic human rights and so, until we help people flee poverty and destitution, we will not see true peace in the world.

At the end, I pray with all my heart that mankind forsakes greed and forgoes the pursuit of narrow self-interests and instead, focuses on relieving the pain and anguish of those who are suffering in the world.

With these words, I would like to once again thank you for joining us here this evening. Thank you very much.

Islam *and* Europe - *A* Clash of Civilisations?

ADLON KEMPINSKI HOTEL
Berlin, Germany
22 OCTOBER 2019

"Gabriel impressed upon me kind treatment towards the neighbour (so much), that I thought he would confer upon him the right of inheritance."

— The Holy Prophet Muhammad[sa]

Islam *and* Europe -
A Clash of Civilisations?

Bismillahir Rahmanir Raheem – in the Name of Allah, the Gracious, Ever Merciful. All distinguished guests, *Assalamo Alaikum Wa Rahmatullahe Wa Barakatohu* – peace and blessings of Allah be upon you all.

First of all, I would like to take this opportunity to thank all of our guests who have accepted our invitation and joined us here this evening. In the world today, particularly in Western and developed nations, there is a great deal of heated debate about immigration and its effect on societies. Much of the debate centres around Muslims – because a view has developed that there is an unbridgeable divide between Muslims and other members of society.

Certain governments and members of the public fear a

clash of civilisations and believe that Muslims are a threat to their society and cannot integrate into the Western world.

Before responding to this contention, it is important to define what exactly is meant by civilisation? In this regard, I present the definition given by the Second Head of the Ahmadiyya Muslim Community, which I fully concur with.[1]

According to the definition, civilisation is the material progress and development of a society. Factors that indicate the strength of a civilisation include its economic progress, the level of technological innovation, the advancement of the means of travel, communication and the intellectual progress of the society. For example, modern forms of communication and transportation are one marker of the level of civilisation, as are its financial system, its economy, its law and order, its trade and industry, the standards of its scientific and academic research and its overall educational standards.

Furthermore, the efforts of a nation to foster peace and stability, whether by virtue of its law enforcement and military proficiency, or by other means, is also a measure of its civilisation.

Separate and distinct from civilisation is a nation's culture. Culture is a manifestation of the views of a people, their attitudes towards social issues and their practices, and instead of being based on material progress, culture is rooted in morality and the religious values and traditions of a nation.

Thus, civilisation is the material, technological and intellectual development of a society, whereas its culture is based on the religious, moral and philosophical make-up of that society.

The difference between civilisation and culture can be easily understood if we look back to the early period of Christianity. At that time, the Roman Empire was at the peak of its powers and, even now, it is considered as one of the greatest civilisations in the history of the world. Due to their material prosperity, urbanisation and the way its territories were governed, the Romans were considered to be tremendously civilised and educated.

However, their sophistication did not equate to higher standards of morality; rather, it was during the early period of Christianity that their people were infused with a progressive culture. Christianity gave people guiding principles based on religion and morality, whilst the Romans prescribed worldly laws and limits.

Hence, the progress and advancement of the Romans reflected their great civilisation, whereas Christianity gave the people a laudable culture. Over time, Christianity became the predominant religion of the Roman Empire and so, the culture it established was adopted by a great civilisation. Allied together, their supreme influence laid the foundations for the values and traditions that remain today in the West.

Whilst people in the West are moving away from religion,

the basic moral values that underpin Western society remain those given by Christianity.

Regarding the debate about immigration, in recent decades, the demographics of several Western countries has altered. Immigrants have arrived from many countries, but it has been the influx of Muslims that has caused most concern and alarm. Many indigenous people fear that mass immigration from Muslim countries threatens their civilisation, culture and values, which have existed for many centuries.

As I have explained, we consider civilisation to be the material progress and advancement of society and rather than disapprove, oppose or deny the growth and development in the West, developing nations seek to emulate it. As a result, rather than Western civilisation being cast aside, we are seeing the opposite.

Due to the modern means of travel and communication, the world has become a global village. The advent of television, mass media and particularly the internet have meant that nothing now remains hidden in the world and so, people who live in economically deprived countries can see how those in affluent nations live. They are being influenced by Western civilisation and desire to attain similar levels of material advancement and innovation.

Thus, the assertion that Western or European civilisation is threatened by the presence of Muslims does not hold water; rather, Western civilisation is influencing other parts of the world and this includes the Muslim world. On the other hand, a fear that the religious and moral culture of the West could be threatened if Islam spreads in Europe is a more legitimate concern, and I shall now address this point.

Firstly, it is undeniable that people are rapidly moving away from religion and this trend is particularly acute in the West. In Western countries, whenever a census is conducted it shows that people are less and less inclined towards religion or belief in God. Given this, I believe that the rapid increase of atheism is a far greater threat to Western culture than Islam. Western values are centuries old and are based upon its religious traditions, and especially on its Christian and Jewish heritage. However, these religious values and cultural norms are under attack from those who oppose all forms of religion and faith.

So, as a Muslim leader, I believe you should protect your heritage and culture by focusing your energies on arresting the decline in religion and bringing people back towards faith and belief, whether that be Christianity, Judaism or any other. It should not be that in the name of advancement, those values and moral standards that have been part of society for many centuries are suddenly abandoned.

I also believe that the decline in religion in the West is the main reason people fear Islam, because they know that, broadly speaking, Muslims remain attached to their faith. In light of this, I wish to make it clear that, despite what you hear or read in the media, there is no cause to fear Islam. Muslims believe the Holy Qur'an to be a final and perfect religious teaching, and it is due to our love and obedience to the Holy Qur'an that we firmly believe that religion is a matter of the heart and personal to every individual.

In chapter 2, verse 257, the Holy Qur'an has categorically stated that there should be no compulsion in matters of religion. Therefore, there is no need for non-Muslims to fear that Muslims will try to forcefully spread their beliefs or impose their views on this part of the world. The hateful ideology of the tiny minority of so-called Muslims who have adopted extremism bears no correlation with the teachings of the Holy Qur'an. Indeed, I have said many times that governments and the relevant authorities should deal very firmly with extremists, be they Muslims or non-Muslims.

In terms of the Ahmadiyya Muslim Community, we believe that under no circumstances does Islam permit the use of force, or any type of coercion, in the spread of faith. Why then is there a need to fear Islam? Why do people think that their civilisation or culture is at risk from Muslims?

Now, after explaining the differences between civilisation and culture from an Islamic perspective, I would like to present some of the core teachings of Islam. Many myths and misconceptions about Islam and its Founder (peace and blessings of Allah be upon him) have spread, and whilst it is not possible to cover all aspects of Islamic teachings in the short time available, I would like to mention some of the rights of mankind that Islam has established.

A very significant verse of the Holy Qur'an, in terms of human rights, is chapter 4, verse 37 which states:

"And worship Allah and associate naught with Him, and show kindness to parents, and to kindred, and orphans, and the needy, and to the neighbour who is a kinsman and the neighbour who is a stranger, and the companion by your side, and the wayfarer and those whom your right hands possess…"

In this verse, where Allah the Almighty instructs Muslims to worship Him, He also instructs them to treat their parents with love and affection. How can this teaching, requiring Muslims to love and honour their parents clash with any religion or nation? How can such a teaching undermine Western society? The verse also requires Muslims to treat their relatives and loved ones with kindness and consideration. It requires them to support and comfort the most vulnerable and under-privileged members of society, such as orphans.

In this regard, we believe that one of the key ways to help the poor is through education. If younger members of society, who are from broken homes or who are stricken by poverty are educated, it will enable them to break free from the shackles of destitution. Opportunities will open up to them and so, free from frustration and resentment, such youths will grow to be productive members of society, rather than being lured towards a life of crime or gang culture. This is why, the Ahmadiyya Muslim Community lays great emphasis on education and within our limited resources, we have built schools in various African countries and fund scholarships for students who cannot afford higher education.

We also believe that rich countries should help the weaker nations of the world build solid foundations. If poorer countries can build up their economies and infrastructures, their people will have opportunities at home and have far less reason to migrate abroad. If their nations are stable and prosperous, it naturally follows that the region and the wider world will benefit.

In the aforementioned verse of the Holy Qur'an, special mention is made to fulfilling the rights of one's neighbours, whether they are Muslim or non-Muslims, and it defines the scope of neighbours to be extremely wide. The Prophet of Islam (peace and blessings of Allah be upon him) said that God Almighty had emphasised the rights of neighbours so strongly that he came to think neighbours would be included amongst a person's rightful heirs.[2] Furthermore, in Islam, neighbours are not only those who live nearby but also those who live further afield, travel companions, work colleagues, subordinates and many other people besides. In effect, Allah the Almighty has made it a moral imperative for Muslims to fulfil the rights of all members of society.

The Founder of Islam (peace and blessings of Allah be upon him) also taught that a person who is not grateful to his fellow human beings, cannot be grateful to Allah the Almighty.[3] What a beautiful principle! Thus, it is necessary that alongside the worship of God, a Muslim must fulfil the rights of humanity.

Again, I would ask how can such a teaching be a threat to Western civilisation? These Islamic teachings are the means of cultivating peace and stability in society, and can only help advance economic output and social development.

Hence, in my view, it is counter-productive for Western people to suggest that Islam or Muslims have no place in this part of the world.

If Muslims come here seeking to integrate, to fulfil the rights of neighbours and strive for the peace and betterment of society, then surely this is something to praise, rather than to condemn or castigate.

Moving on, some people argue or believe that Muslims are instructed to perform Jihad, and so they fear they will come to the West and wage a violent war seeking to enforce an Islamic civilisation and culture, and shatter the peace of society. This is based on a clear misunderstanding of what Jihad is and why religious wars were fought in the early period of Islam. Islam is not a bloodthirsty or violent religion.

During the early period of Islam, the Muslims were forced to defend themselves after war was waged upon them and so, a companion of the Holy Prophet Muhammad (peace and blessings of Allah be upon him) asked to join the Muslim army so he could take part in Jihad. The Prophet of Islam (peace and blessings of Allah be upon him) rejected his plea and said that, because his parents were in a fragile state, he should remain at home, care for them and consider that to be his Jihad.[4] If the objective of Jihad was conquest, bloodshed and warfare, the Prophet of Islam (peace and blessings of Allah be upon him) would surely have taken up his offer and sought to bolster the Muslim army.

I should clarify that, whilst it is true that Muslim armies fought in some religious wars during the early period of Islam, the purpose was never to overpower, oppress or compel people to accept Islam. Those wars were fought to protect the institution of religion and uphold the principle of freedom of belief.

In chapter 22, verses 40-41, the Holy Qur'an very clearly states that if the aggressors were not stopped, all churches, synagogues, temples, mosques and other places of worship would be under grave threat, as the underlying intention of the disbelievers of Makkah was to destroy all traces of religion from the face of the earth. This proves that Islam protects all religions.

Then, with regard to bringing up our children, chapter 6

verse 152 of the Holy Qur'an states that Muslims must not *"slay their children"*. This commandment instructs Muslims to nourish their children with love and affection, to morally guide them and to educate them so that they grow to become highly competent and moral individuals who are assets to their community and nation.

Similarly, Islam has taught Muslims to defend the rights of vulnerable members of society. For example, in chapter 4, verse 7 of the Qur'an, Muslims are obliged to protect orphan children from exploitation and to guard their inheritance with integrity, until they reach an age where they can manage it themselves.

Furthermore, another very common allegation in the Western world is that Muslims do not respect women or their rights. First of all, it should be noted that Islam was the first religion to give women the right to inherit, the right to divorce and various other rights. In addition, Islam emphasises the vast importance of educating girls and giving them opportunities for personal growth and development. Not a single girl or woman should ever be deprived of education or discriminated against in any respect.

In an era, when the rights of women and girls were routinely disregarded, and they were regarded as inferior to boys, the Prophet of Islam (peace and blessings of Allah be upon him) brought a revolution in the cause of women's rights.

He instructed Muslims to love, cherish and respect their daughters and to never consider them lesser to their sons.

Moreover, in a famous saying, the Holy Prophet of Islam (peace and blessings of Allah be upon him) said that *"paradise lies under the feet of one's mother"*.[5] These words illustrate the momentous role women play in society and their unique and distinguished status in society.

Primarily, it is the role of mothers to nurture their children through their formative years and so, they play the leading role in ensuring that the coming generations grow into morally upstanding citizens who contribute to their society. Mothers are the people who have the power and influence to turn their nations into a heaven on earth and who can unlock the doors to an eternal paradise for their children.

Furthermore, in chapter 4, verse 20, the Holy Qur'an has stated that Muslim men must treat their wives lovingly and respectfully. In Western countries, not a day goes by without reports of the police or the courts being forced to intervene and deal with horrifying cases of domestic abuse. Various studies and reports, such as the 2018 report by the Office for National Statistics in the UK, prove that such crimes are not linked to any religion and another recent report has shown that the same is true here in Germany. Thus, it is entirely unjust to brand Islam as a misogynistic religion.

As I have outlined, Islam is a religion that bestows honour and dignity upon women and any man who treats a woman cruelly is guilty of grievously violating Islam's teachings.

Islam also requires its followers to respect the religious sentiments and beliefs of other people. The Covenant of Madinah was a true illustration of this teaching where the Torah was recognised and respected as the law-bearing book of the Jews.

Islam has even established the rights of a person's enemies and opponents, whereby chapter 2, verse 191 of the Holy Qur'an states that no injustice or transgression should be done against one's enemy, even during a state of war. Regrettably, in today's world, which proudly boasts of being more civilised and advanced than any previous era, individuals and countries disregard the rights of their opponents as a matter of routine, and perpetrate huge cruelties and waste no opportunity for revenge.

In chapter 5, verse 9 of the Holy Qur'an, Allah the Almighty has proclaimed that the enmity of a nation or people should never incite a person to sacrifice the principles of justice and equity; rather, Islam teaches that in all circumstances, no matter how challenging, you must remain firmly attached to the principles of justice and integrity and never be motivated by a desire for vengeance.

As a result of this magnificent teaching, we see the unparalleled example of grace, compassion and mercy exhibited by the Holy Prophet Muhammad (peace and blessings of Allah be upon him) at the time of the Victory of Makkah.

History proves that Muslims were killed, plundered and tortured in Makkah and ultimately, they were driven out of their homes and had to migrate.

Yet when he returned victoriously to Makkah and the entire city was under his command, his first pronouncement was that no revenge would be taken from those who had brutally persecuted the Muslims. At that moment of triumph, the Holy Prophet Muhammad (peace and blessings of Allah be upon him) exhibited supreme humility and forbearance.

He declared that, in accordance with Islam's teachings, all those who had tormented the Muslims were to be instantly forgiven and that nobody would be treated unjustly, regardless of whether they accepted Islam or not.

Another moral revolution in favour of the weakest members of society brought by Islam regarded slavery, which prior to Islam, was rampant and considered a normal part of society. Upon the command of Allah the Almighty, the Prophet of Islam (peace and blessings of Allah be upon him) sought to bring an end to this practice.

Thus, in chapter 24, verse 34 the Holy Qur'an states that if a slave seeks freedom, he should be released and if certain fiscal dues are levied, they must be reasonable and payable in small, easily manageable instalments or be waived altogether.

As I said, during that era, slavery was part and parcel of society and so, by calling for their emancipation, the Prophet of Islam (peace and blessings of Allah be upon him) brought about a sea-change in attitudes.

In today's world, physical slavery no longer exists, but it has been replaced by economic bondage and servitude, wherein the relationship between the most powerful nations on earth and weaker countries has become akin to the relationship of a master and a slave. For example, loans disguised as aid-packages are given by rich countries to weaker nations who have no option but to accept whatever strings are attached.

Invariably, the crippling levels of interest mean that the short-term loans lead to long-term misery and liability. The end result is that the defaulting country has no choice but to bend to the will of the dominant nation. Such slavery is utterly immoral.

From the outset, Islam also established the rights of non-Muslims and counselled Muslims to show restraint for the sake of the peace and unity of society. For example, in chapter 6, verse 109, the Holy Qur'an declares that Muslims should not even speak against the idols of non-religious people, because it could provoke them to speak against Allah the Almighty.

Thus, to ensure tensions are not inflamed and to protect society from a vicious cycle of hatred and hostility, Muslims have been instructed to show patience at all times.

In the short time available, I have mentioned only a few points that illustrate the rights of humanity that have been established by Islam. I hope what I have said will have reassured you that Islam is not a threat to Western civilisation or its culture. If there are any Muslims who usurp the rights of non-Muslims, it is only because they reject Islam's teachings or are wholly ignorant of them. They dishonour Islam and serve only to defame its pure name.

In conclusion, it is clear we are living in a world that is on tenterhooks and I fear the precarious situation we are facing could escalate at any time. People must realise that words can have far-reaching consequences and so, rather than speaking of a clash of civilisations, or needlessly ratcheting up tensions between different communities, people should refrain from attacking the religious teachings of one another.

Instead of seeking to place restrictions upon the expressions of faith, we should recognise that we are all part of one human race more connected than ever before. We should embrace our diversity and focus on establishing unity so that long-term peace can develop in the world.

However, currently we are seeing the opposite. Muslim and non-Muslim countries alike are putting their own interests ahead of the interests of the wider world, and are crossing all limits of fairness and morality in pursuit of their goals. Reminiscent of the dark days of the past, opposing blocs and alliances are forming and it seems as though the world is hell-bent on inviting its destruction.

Today, there are a host of countries who have acquired

nuclear bombs or other destructive weapons that have the potential to destroy civilisation as we know it. Who is to say that these weapons will never be used or will not end up in the wrong hands? All it takes is one miscalculation or misstep for hostilities to trigger the unthinkable. The consequences of such a war are incomprehensible, but it is safe to say that the world will never be the same again. If nuclear weapons are ever used, it will not just be us who bear the consequences; rather, our children and future generations will have to suffer for our sins. Generations of children will be born with intellectual and physical disabilities and have their hopes and dreams shattered through no fault of their own.

Is that the parting legacy we wish to bequeath to those who follow us? Surely not! Thus, instead of fanning flames of hatred, whether based on religious or ethnic differences or for political objectives, we must recognise the warning signs and change our ways before it is too late. Let us all, irrespective of our differences, join together and work with a spirit of mutual respect, tolerance and affection for the peace of the world and to promote freedom of belief.

May Allah grant wisdom and intelligence to those who are causing conflict in the name of religion and may peace and justice prevail – Ameen. With these words, I would like to thank you once again for joining us this evening. Thank you very much.

Ahmadi Muslim Researchers - Restoring Islam's *Golden* Age

AHMADIYYA MUSLIM RESEARCH
ASSOCIATION CONFERENCE
Islamabad, Tilford, UK
14 DECEMBER 2019

"The superiority of the learned man over the devout is like that of the moon, on the night when it is full, over the rest of the stars. The learned are the heirs of the Prophets"

— The Holy Prophet Muhammad[sa]

Ahmadi Muslim Researchers - Restoring Islam's *Golden* Age

After reciting Tashahhud, Ta'awwuz and Bismillah [the Islamic manner of beginning an address] Hazrat Mirza Masroor Ahmad[aba], Worldwide Head of the Ahmadiyya Muslim Community and Fifth Khalifah said:

اِنَّ فِىۡ خَلۡقِ السَّمٰوٰتِ وَالۡاَرۡضِ وَاخۡتِلَافِ الَّيۡلِ وَ النَّهَارِ لَاٰيٰتٍ لِّاُولِى الۡاَلۡبَابِ ○ الَّذِيۡنَ يَذۡكُرُوۡنَ اللّٰهَ قِيَامًا وَّ قُعُوۡدًا وَّ عَلٰى جُنُوۡبِهِمۡ وَيَتَفَكَّرُوۡنَ فِىۡ خَلۡقِ السَّمٰوٰتِ وَالۡاَرۡضِ ۚ رَبَّنَا مَا خَلَقۡتَ هٰذَا بَاطِلًا ۚ سُبۡحٰنَكَ فَقِنَا عَذَابَ النَّارِ ○

These verses of the Holy Qur'an I have just recited are verses 191-192 of Surah Aal-e-'Imran and the translation is as follows:

"In the creation of the heavens and the earth and in the alternation of the night and the day there are indeed Signs for men of understanding. Those who remember Allah while standing, sitting, and lying on their sides, and ponder over the creation of the heavens and the earth: 'Our Lord, Thou hast not created this in vain; nay, Holy art Thou; save us, then, from the punishment of the Fire.'"

Today, with the Grace of Allah, you are holding the first International AMRA Conference. I hope and pray that the event has proven beneficial and a source of learning for all of the participants.

In many verses of the Holy Qur'an, including those just recited, Allah the Almighty has mentioned the creation of the heavens and the earth and He has instructed us to reflect upon the true purpose of our creation. He has encouraged us to use our brains, to ponder upon His creation and to search for new roads of human progress and innovation, through research and reflection. Indeed, Allah the Almighty has deemed humans as the *"best of creation"* [1] because of the fact that we have been granted intelligence and understanding. We have been granted the ability to differentiate between right and wrong. We have been given the ability to think and comprehend. Unique amongst all creation, Allah the Almighty has given mankind the insight to appreciate that whatever He has created has been made for our benefit, on condition that we use it in the right way.

Certainly, out of all the heavenly scriptures, the Holy Qur'an is unique in terms of the vast amount of insight it has given about the universe and its inception, and how it has encouraged scientific research and the pursuit of knowledge. In this regard, the Promised Messiah[as] [Hazrat Mirza Ghulam Ahmad of Qadian] has stated that when a believer studies and ponders over the celestial bodies and the entire universe, it causes their minds to open up and for them to become enlightened. The result is that they are led towards a firm belief in the existence of God Almighty, as they see the signs and evidence for His existence all around them.[2]

On the other hand, the interests of worldly and non-religious researchers are finite and narrow. When they study something, they assess it in a limited way. However, a righteous person is not satisfied by merely identifying the dimensions of the world, its material form or calculating the gravitational forces. Nor are they content by simply determining the main characteristics of the sun, the moon and the stars; rather, a true believer will continually strive and struggle to observe and understand the perfect harmony of nature and the world around us. He or she will have an unquenchable thirst to identify the hidden characteristics or potential of the physical world, and as they realise its brilliance and perfection, they will inevitably be drawn towards their Creator, and their faith in the existence of God Almighty will be enhanced. Consequently, when an intelligent person reflects carefully upon the heavens and the earth, the universe and why the length of the night and day remains constantly in a state of flux, it causes them to perceive God Almighty and appreciate His perfect creation. When they see God Almighty in this way and recognise His majesty, they turn towards Him with increased fervency and passion, and seek His Help and Grace in their efforts to further understand and unlock the mysteries of the universe. In order to attain His blessings and help, they remember Him whilst standing, sitting and resting, just as it has been described as the state of a righteous believer in the verses of the Holy Qur'an recited. When they pray to Allah for guidance, He grants them clarity of thought, He enlightens their minds and washes away the haze of incomprehension that previously existed. He grants them an understanding of the universe and planets and they come to recognise with certainty, that such a perfect and precise natural order could never have come about by chance or on its own; rather, it is a reflection and indicator of a Great Creator. Indeed, it is a testament to the existence of a Universal Creator.

Those people, whose minds are opened in this way, bow down before their Creator and pray that they are saved from His Wrath, and that He guides them towards prosperity and a deeper understanding of His creation.

In a similar vein, the Promised Messiah[as] has stated that the continued study of physics, astronomy and the sciences will always lead a righteous person towards God Almighty. The more they learn about God's creation and the world around them, the more they will appreciate the beauty of Allah the Almighty through the wonders of the universe.[3]

Once a believer gains such knowledge and insight, he or she is not just able to guide others about the latest scientific developments, rather they will also be tooled with the armoury to prove to the world the existence of that One God, who is the Creator of all creation. This is the symbol of a true believer, the means of their success and their path to attaining real honour and prestige in the world.

It was in this way, reflecting upon the universe, that Professor Dr Abdus Salam Sahib spent his life and he used whatever insight he gained as evidence to prove the existence of God.

Hence, all Ahmadi researchers or academics should continually keep in view the Oneness of God Almighty before, during and after conducting any research or study. They should seek to conduct their investigations with the firm intention of eliciting evidence that will enable them to prove the existence of the One God to sceptics and disbelievers, and to refute those who claim that science and religion are irreconcilable. When they research in this way and seek the Help of Allah the Almighty at each step, no doubt He will assist them at every juncture and be their guiding light.

As I said before, the research of a secular person is based on a purely worldly approach and they use their intellect for the sake of material progress. Their efforts can lead to scientific advancement, but the research of a believer has a far greater potential impact. Their research will not only lead to scientific progress and the development of modern technologies, but will also serve to offer proof of the existence of God Almighty.

Therefore, Ahmadi Muslim researchers, especially those who pursue the sciences, should not only have the intention of enhancing the understanding of their chosen field, but should also maintain an everlasting resolve to find proofs of the existence of God. As I have said, this was how Dr Abdus Salam Sahib conducted his work and he attained phenomenal success as a result.

Remember, that the Promised Messiah[as] has said that people of true intellect and wisdom are those who never forget God Almighty and always remember Him.

Thus, where our scientists and researchers strive to excel in their academic pursuits, they must always safeguard their faith, fulfil the rights of Allah the Almighty and fulfil the demands laid upon them to search for additional evidence proving the existence of an All-Powerful God. Hence, there should always be a clear distinction between Ahmadi scientists and researchers, and others who pursue similar fields of study. And the difference ought to be that the pursuit of knowledge of an Ahmadi must be based upon *Taqwa* – righteousness.

Indeed, the Holy Prophet of Islam[sa] said that a person should fear the acumen and perceptive nature of a believer, because their knowledge is based upon righteousness.[4]

In summary, the love and majesty of Allah the Almighty should be forever ingrained and imprinted in your hearts and minds. If you research and seek to evolve your work in this way, then Allah the Almighty will bestow upon you great success, *Insha'Allah* [if Allah wills].

Some of you may be aware that once, a well-known Western researcher and traveller, Professor Clement Wragge, travelled to Qadian to meet the Promised Messiah[as]. During their conversation, the Promised Messiah[as] explained that Allah the Almighty has created the sun and the moon, the stars and planets to serve human beings and for the benefit of humankind.[5] In light of this, whilst conducting research to answer questions that remain unsolved, an Ahmadi researcher must keep at the forefront of their mind that whatever has been created by Allah the Almighty has been made for the benefit of humanity. It should be their objective to uncover and derive the benefits and to ensure that whatever intellectual progress is made is utilised in the right way for the betterment of mankind.

In his discussions with Professor Wragge, the Promised Messiah[as] affirmed that there was no contradiction between science and religion and that no matter how far science progressed, it would never prove a single letter or word of the Holy Qur'an, or the teachings of Islam, to be untrue. Rather, every discovery and every development would serve as additional proof of the truth of the teachings of the Holy Qur'an and the existence of the One God.

Certainly, the Holy Qur'an does not shy away from science or discourage its followers from study. Quite the opposite – the Holy Qur'an instructs believers to explore, to investigate and to utilise their intellect and God-given faculties.[6]

Indeed, those who strive to advance human knowledge for the benefit of humanity will reap the rewards of Allah the Almighty for their efforts.

However, the Holy Qur'an has also warned humans from interfering with the laws of nature or from seeking to change or modify the creation of Allah through unnatural means.[7] For example, in recent years, the boundaries of scientific ethics have gradually eroded, whereby there have been attempts to pursue immoral and dangerous pursuits such as genetic engineering and the cloning of living creatures. The results of such undertakings, where humans far exceed their limits and seek to "play God", will surely be catastrophic and be the means of driving mankind towards its destruction. It will not only lead the protagonists towards Hell in the

Hereafter, but they will also be responsible for creating a living Hell on earth.

This is something every Ahmadi Muslim researcher and scientist must guard against. You must only pursue those avenues that are for the benefit of humanity and which are according to the limits prescribed by Allah the Almighty. Always remember that to stay within the confines of the Holy Qur'an is the hallmark of a believer.

If you conduct your work in this way, you can achieve great things and revive the once distinguished reputation of Muslim scholars and academics.

With the Grace of Allah, during the Middle Ages, countless Muslim scientists, philosophers and intellectuals left an indelible mark on humanity by advancing the cause of human knowledge and understanding. Their pioneering efforts brought about a remarkable revolution in the world and their research and discoveries continue to be the basis for modern science and mathematics. They utilised their God-given talents and faculties, whilst seeking the Help of Allah the Almighty and reflecting upon His creation, and as a result, have been recognised through history and continue to be acknowledged and respected today.

For example, an article published by the National Geographic in 2016 titled *How early Islamic Science advanced Medicine*, identifies the contributions of Muslim scientists in the early period of Islam. The article states:

"Physicians from Islamic countries during the late Middle Ages enjoyed great respect. Their reputation was well deserved, for the study and practice of medicine was then led by Muslim societies across their immense territory, which extended from modern-day southern Spain to Iran." [8]

It further states:

"By the 900s, drawing from a growing body of Greek, Persian, and Sanskrit works translated into Arabic, Islamic medicine quickly became the most sophisticated in the world. Christians, Jews, Hindus, and scholars from many other traditions, looked to Arabic as a language of science. Doctors of different faiths worked together, debating and studying with Arabic as the common tongue." [9]

The article continues:

"The brightest star in the Baghdad firmament was undoubtedly the extraordinary Ibn Sina…Already a doctor at age 18, his great volume Al-Qanun fi al-Tibb – Canon of Medicine – became one of the most famous medical works of all time… [Ibn Sina's] attempt to harmonize the medical practices of the Greek thinker Galen with the philosophy of Aristotle reveals the multiple nature of the debt owed to Muslim scholarship, which did not merely revive Greek authors, but stimulated new patterns

of thought for the centuries ahead. The reconciling of practical science, thought, and religion ensured Canon was studied by European medics until the 18th century." [10]

Moreover, the National Geographic article labels the period of Muslim rule in Spain as a *"period of scholarly development"* and describes Cordoba in the 10th Century as the *"most cultured city in Europe"* and *"a great centre of study and exploration."*

In another article, published by The New York Times, *How Islam Won, and Lost, the Lead in Science* the contribution of early Muslim scientists is also openly praised. The author writes:

"Civilisations don't just clash...they can learn from each other. Islam is a good example of that...The intellectual meeting of Arabia and Greece was one of the greatest events in history... Its scale and consequences are enormous, not just for Islam but for Europe and the world." [11]

However, the article also notes that many of the contributions made by the early Muslims were not preserved. In this regard, it states:

"Historians say they still know very little about this golden age. Few of the major scientific works from that era have been

translated from Arabic and thousands of manuscripts have never even been read by modern scholars." [12]

Hence, the historic contributions of Muslim scholars is unquestioned. Yet, most regrettably, the recent intellectual state of much of the Muslim world has been lamentable.

Over time, as Muslims moved away from God Almighty and the qualities associated with a believer diminished rapidly amongst them, the Muslims — who had previously led the world in science and research — gradually moved to an age of intellectual ignorance that persists to this day. Instead of continuing to be the leaders of innovation and discovery, the period of Muslim academic enlightenment drew to an end and the Muslims relied on the discoveries and modern technologies made by others. Instead of being those who gave to the world, the Muslims became those who only took. As a result, where the world recognises the outstanding historic contribution of Muslims to science and learning, it considers the intellectual status of the modern-day Muslim world to be woeful. The truth is that, generally speaking, the Muslim world has lost its passion for education and pushing the boundaries of human knowledge. Muslim nations have become immersed in the luxuries and comforts of the world and so, they no longer have the drive or motivation to toil in the pursuit of knowledge or to reflect upon the universe.

The failure of the contemporary Muslim world to excel

in science and learning has been discussed by Hillel Ofek, a Research Fellow at the Clements Centre for National Security in the United States, in an article titled *Why the Arabic World turned away from Science*[13]. He describes how Muslims have gone from leading the world in science and the development of human civilisation to a state where their contributions are now mocked amongst the academic community. He quotes a professor of history who notes that until around the year 1600, *"nothing in Europe could hold a candle"* to the intellectual advancement made by Muslim scientists and scholars. Furthermore, he notes how many scientific and mathematical terms, such as algebra, algorithm, alchemy and alkali derive from Arabic and reflect Islam's contribution to the world. Yet he goes on to paint a modern-day picture of science in the Muslim world that is completely at odds with its illustrious past. For example, he notes that there have only ever been two scientists from Muslim countries who have won the Nobel Prize, despite the fact there are approximately 1.6 billion Muslims in the world.

Another stark statistic he presents is that 46 Muslim countries combined contributed just one percent of the world's scientific literature.

In a similar vein, he states that in 1989, the United States published over 10,000 scientific papers that were frequently cited, whilst in the entire Arab world just four commonly cited papers were published in the same period.

He also notes how between 1980 and 2000, just one country, South Korea, granted over 16,000 intellectual patents, whilst nine Arab countries, including Egypt, Saudi Arabia and the UAE granted a combined total of just 370.

The article also quotes the Nobel Laureate, Professor Steven Weinberg, speaking about the dearth of scientific material originating from Muslim countries. Professor Weinberg states:

"Though there are talented scientists of Muslim origin working productively in the West, for forty years I have not seen a single paper by a physicist or astronomer working in a Muslim country that was worth reading." [14]

Thus, in intellectual and scientific terms, Muslims and the Islamic nations have gone from leading the world, to being treated with scorn and derision.

At this time of intellectual ignorance amongst the Islamic world, it is the great challenge for Ahmadi Muslim scientists and researchers to revive the honour and dignity of Islam in the global academic arena. Indeed, it should be your ambition to take up the glorious mantle of enlightenment adorned by the great Muslim scholars and inventors of the Middle Ages.

Each year, it is a tradition that our Jama'at [Ahmadiyya Muslim Community] awards gold medals for outstanding educational achievement in various fields. However, when the scheme was initiated by Hazrat Khalifatul-Masih III[rh] [Hazrat Mirza Nasir Ahmad, Third Caliph and Worldwide Head of the Ahmadiyya Muslim Community], he instructed that the gold medals and scholarships were specifically to reward those who excelled in science. He started the scheme shortly after Dr Abdus Salam Sahib won the Nobel Prize, and it was his ardent desire that at least 100 Ahmadi Muslims would soon follow in the footsteps of Dr Abdus Salam and become eminent scientists by the time our Jama'at [Ahmadiyya Muslim Community] entered its second century. Three decades of the second century of Ahmadiyyat have now passed and regrettably, I do not think we have even produced a scientist who has become world-renowned in that time.

In addition, for the past thirteen or fourteen years, I have instructed Ahmadi students either directly, or through Majlis Khuddamul Ahmadiyya [Ahmadiyya Muslim Youth Association], to enter the field of academia and research, and to endeavour to reach the highest echelons of their fields. However, so far, it cannot be said that the results have been anywhere near as good as I had hoped. As far as I know, hardly any Ahmadi has played an outstanding or extraordinary role in the scientific and intellectual development of the world.

Here I would also like to appreciate the efforts of the USA Chapter of the Association of Ahmadi Scientists, who are somehow active and hold regular meetings on science and the Qur'an. Yet, we cannot say they have achieved that exceptional mark expected of them.

Consequently, having gathered here and held this conference, you must all consider it your mission to pursue excellence within your chosen field. You must leave here with a firm determination in your hearts to follow in the footsteps of Dr Abdus Salam and those outstanding Muslim scholars and researchers, who left behind a rich legacy of knowledge many centuries ago. You must reflect upon how you can develop a greater understanding of the world and develop new technologies or systems through which humanity can benefit.

As scientists and researchers, it is up to you to exercise your minds and talents to seek out the ways and methods to accomplish great feats of learning.

You should stay in contact with one another and particularly with those who are working in similar areas of research and learn from each other. Through mutual discussion and coordination, you may be able to achieve better results.

Work with diligence, passion and above all, constantly seek the Help of Allah the Almighty at every step of your academic journey and keep His Majesty at the forefront of your minds.

With these words, I pray that may Allah the Almighty enable you to flourish and to achieve great success in your fields of expertise. And may we soon come to witness the dawn of a new Islamic golden age of intellectual progress and advancement, led by Ahmadi Muslims across the world – Ameen.

About the Ahmadiyya Muslim Youth Association

Majlis Khuddamul Ahmadiyya, or the Ahmadiyya Muslim Youth Association (AMYA) was established by His Holiness Mirza Bashiruddin Mahmood Ahmad, Khalifatul-Masih II[ra], in 1938 in Qadian, India. AMYA exists as an auxiliary of the Ahmadiyya Muslim Community around the world for men between the ages of 16 and 40; a sub-organisation within AMYA is dedicated to boys between the ages of 7 and 15. In the UK, AMYA has a membership of over 9,000 young British Muslims; it is the UK's oldest Muslim youth organisation.

AMYA UK is committed to the spiritual, moral, social, intellectual and physical development of young Muslims and holds regular programmes to this end. These include academic and sporting activities as well as a mixture of charitable and social welfare efforts. The purpose of AMYA's activities is to train young men with the ultimate aim of creating a living relationship with God and serving mankind, irrespective of people's beliefs, race or background. The Islamic motto *Love for All, Hatred for None* underpins this ethos.

AMYA UK's central headquarters are situated in Farnham, Surrey. AMYA UK has more than 150 branches across the country and is a self-funded organisation, relying on donations from its members.

The founder of the Ahmadiyya Muslim Community, Hazrat Mirza Ghulam Ahmad - the Promised Messiah[as] stated:

"My purpose, yearning and heartfelt desire is to serve humanity. This is my job, this is my faith, this is my habit and this is my way of life."

The youth not only draw inspiration and strength from this profound message, but also strive to practically live up to this in their every day life.

Notes

TERRORISM WAS NEVER JUSTIFIED BY THE HOLY PROPHET MUHAMMAD[SA]

1   Dodd, V. (2016). "Isis planning 'enormous and spectacular attacks', anti-
    terror chief warns". *The Guardian.* 7 March 2016
2   Jones. O (2015). "Islamophobia plays right into the hands of Isis". *The
    Guardian.* 25 November 2015
3   Considine, C. 2016. "Religious Pluralism and Civic Rights in a 'Muslim
    Nation': An Analysis of Prophet Muhammad's Covenants with Christians".
    Religions, 7(2), p.15
4   The Holy Qur'an 1:2-3
5   Sahih Bukhari, Kitab-ul-Mazalim, Book 46, Chapter 4, Hadith 5
6   The Holy Qur'an 42:41
7   ibid, 18:30
8   Hazrat Mirza Ghulam Ahmad - the Promised Messiah[as], *Tohfa Qaisiriyah*,
    Ruhani Khazain, Volume 12 (2008). p. 281
9   Hazrat Mirza Ghulam Ahmad - the Promised Messiah[as], *Noah's Ark*. Islam
    International Publications, 2018. p. 49
10 The Holy Qur'an 2:139
11 Nasralla, S. (2015). "Austria says fight against Islamic State needs Syria's
    Assad". *Reuters.* 8 September 2015
12 Gray, J. (2015). "Islamist terror, security and the Hobbesian question of

order". *New Statesman*. 26 November 2015 issue

13 Glazer, E. (2015) "U.S. Cut Cash to Iraq on Iran, ISIS Fears". *The Wall Street Journal*. 3 November 2015

14 Al-Khatteeb, L. (2014). "How Iraq's black market in oil funds ISIS". CNN. 22 August 2014

15 Karam, J. (2015). "2015 winner in Middle East: U.S. arms exporters". *Al Arabiya*. 31 December 2015

16 Luce, Dan De. (2015). "Is the U.S. Ready for an Endless War Against the Islamic State?". *Foreign Policy*. 27 August 2015

MUSLIM MIGRANTS & INTEGRATION

1   BBC News (2018) "Sweden rape: Most convicted attackers foreign-born, says TV". 22 August 2018

2   Bisset, V. (2018) "'I met my IS captor on a German street'". *BBC News*. 18 August 2018

3   For example see address delivered by His Holiness Mirza Masroor Ahmad, Khalifatul-Masih V[aba] at the 41st Annual Convention of the Ahmadiyya Muslim Community Germany on 3 September 2016. "Building Bridges of Peace". *The Review of Religions*. 30 October 2016

4   The Holy Qur'an 24:3

5   Out of many such examples see address by His Holiness Mirza Masroor Ahmad[aba] "World in Crisis – How do we Cope?". Delivered 17 May 2016, Stockhold, Sweden. *The Review of Religions*. 30 July 2016

6   Sahih Bukhari, Kitab Al-Zakat, Book 24, Hadith 31

7   For example see Sahih Bukhari, Kitab Manaqibul-Ansar, Book 63, Hadith 5

8   Blond, Josie Le. (2018). "Germany mulls year of national service for young people and migrants". *The Guardian*. 26 August 2018

9   Sunan Nasai, Kitab-ul-Iman Wa Sharaiahu, Book 47, Hadith 11

10 Al Mu'jam Al Kabeer, Juz 2, Page 490

TRUE AND SUSTAINABLE WORLD PEACE

1   Coy, P. (2019). "With Putin and Trump in Charge, the Risk of Nuclear War Returns". *Bloomberg Businessweek*. 31 January 2019

2   ibid.

3   For example see address by His Holiness Mirza Masroor Ahmad[aba] "The Devastating Consequences of a Nuclear War and the Critical Need for Absolute Justice". Delivered 24 March 2012, London, UK. *The Review of Religions*. 21 May 2012

4   Rohr, M. (2018). "'The World Is Changing Dramatically'". *Der Speigel*. 24
    September 2018
5   Gorbachev, M. (2018). "Mikhail Gorbachev: A New Nuclear Arms Race Has
    Begun". *The New York Times*. 25 October 2018
6   ibid.
7   Address delivered by His Holiness Mirza Masroor Ahmad[aba] at the European
    Parliament, 4 December 2012. Published in *The Review of Religions* 28
    February 2013
8   ibid.
9   ibid.
10 The Holy Qur'an 49:10

ISLAMIC PRINCIPLES ON EDUCATION AND SERVING HUMANITY

1   The Holy Qur'an 1:2
2   ibid, 21:108
3   Sahih Bukhari, Kitab Fazail Ashab-un-Nabi, Book 62, Hadith 81
4   See Sahih Bukhari, Kitab-ul-Itq, Book 49
5   Sahih Bukhari, Kitab-ul-Khusomaat, Book 44, Hadith 2
6   The Holy Qur'an 6:109
7   Sahih Bukhari, Kitab-ul-Adab, Book 78, Chapter 134
8   ibid, Kitab-ul-Adab, Book 78, Chapter 131
9   ibid, Kitab-ul-Adab, Book 78, Chapter 28, Hadith 45
10 The Holy Qur'an 22:41
11 ibid, 20:115
12 Overby. D (2001). "How Islam Won, and Lost, the Lead in Science". *The New
    York Times*. 30 October 2001

ISLAM & EUROPE: A CLASH OF CIVILISATIONS

1   His Holiness Mirza Bashiruddin Mahmood Ahmad - Khalifatul-Masih II[ra],
    Introduction to the Study of the Holy Qur'an. Islam International Publications.
    2016. p.14-15
2   Sahih Bukhari, Kitab-ul-Adab, Book 78, Chapter 28, Hadith 45
3   Sunan Abi Dawood, Kitab-ul-Adab, Book 43, Hadith 39
4   Sahih Bukhari, Kitab-ul-Adab, Book 78, Hadith 3
5   Sunan Nasa'i, Kitab-ul-Jihad, Book 25, Hadith 20

1   The Holy Qur'an 17:71
2   Hazrat Mirza Ghulam Ahmad - The Promised Messiah[as], *The Philosophy of the Teachings of Islam*. Islam International Publications, 2017. p186-187
3   Hazrat Mirza Ghulam Ahmad - The Promised Messiah[as], *Surma Chashm-e-Arya*, Ruhani Khazain, Vol 2. Islam International Publications, 2008. p. 191-192
4   Tirmidhi, Kitab-ut-Tafseer, Book 47, Hadith 3419
5   Mufti Muhammad Sadiq, *Zikr-e-Habib*. p. 330
6   The Holy Qur'an 3:191-192
7   ibid, 4:120
8   Bustinza, V. (2016). "How Early Islamic Science Advanced Medicine". *National Geographic History*. November-December 2016
9   ibid.
10 ibid.
11 Overby. D (2001). "How Islam Won, and Lost, the Lead in Science". *The New York Times*. 30 October 2001
12 ibid.
13 Ofek, H. (2011). "Why the Arabic World Turned Away from Science". *The New Atlantis*, Number 30, Winter 2011. p. 3-23
14 ibid.

Index